REC

"To some extent we all have our personal prisons, in our hectic and stress-filled days. This is why Mark Conner's book *Prison Break* is so timely and helpful. Whether your personal prison is one of anger or fear, worry or some destructive habit, addictions or whatever, Mark offers help that can free you from your prison. The book is practical yet sound, both psychologically and biblically, and easy to read. I am sure no reader will be disappointed."

Archibald D. Hart, Ph.D., FPPR.
Senior Professor of Psychology and Dean Emeritus
Graduate School of Psychology
Fuller Theological Seminary
Pasadena, California.

"It has been my privilege to mentor Mark Conner for 'who he is' in his life and ministry for the last four and a half years. I know Mark as an outstanding Christian leader, who has great integrity in life and leadership. Mark therefore is a living example in that he lives in the freedom which is the theme of this book."

Keith Farmer
B.Comm., B.A.(Hons), D.Min., MAPS

"I have known Mark Conner as a friend and 'encourager' for about twenty years. He has an integrity about his personhood and ministry which I admire. He's also very practical - and *Prison Break* reveals how well he's in touch with the ordinary problems we ordinary people face. I highly commend it."

Rowland Croucher
Director, John Mark Ministries
jmm.aaa.net.au

OTHER BOOKS AND RESOURCES
BY MARK CONNER

Transforming Your Church

Successful Christian Ministry

Pass the Baton: Successful Leadership Transition

WEB: www.markconner.com.au

BLOG: www.blog.markconner.com.au

To my daughter
Echo.
Hopefully the
message in this
book helps you as
much as it did me

MARK CONNER

PRISON

BREAK

all my love,
Dad

SPECIAL THANKS

I would like to give my special thanks to:

My best friend Nicole and our three adult
children - Josiah, Natasha and Ashley.
You are the most important people in my life.

My many teachers and mentors who have taught me much
about finding personal freedom.

The leaders, staff, and people I have had the privilege of doing
life and ministry together with over the years.

My Father God for his amazing grace in saving me and calling
me to be part of his purpose on planet earth.

TABLE OF CONTENTS

FOREWORD

Many years ago the church I was pastoring conducted an informal survey with the leaders. One of the open-ended questions we asked them was, "I wish someone would preach about . . ." Needless to say, we received enough ideas and suggestions to keep us busy until Jesus comes back. One of the common threads in the survey results was the desire for more practical teaching on everyday personal issues such as handling depression, anger, fear, and addictions.

As a result, we began to ensure that each year we prepared a practical series of Bible-based messages aimed at helping people work through common personal issues such as these. One of the most popular and beneficial series we have done was called *Prison Break*. A number of other churches have used our material and the messages have had a similar positive effect. I thought that it would be worthwhile putting this material together into a book that hopefully can reach even more people.

This is my first pastoral book as the other three books that I have written are more related to church and leadership matters. I am really excited about this project. I love people and I have a genuine desire to see them grow and change. My prayer is that this material will assist many people in experiencing a prison break in their life so that they are empowered to move into the full freedom that is available because of what Jesus Christ has done for us.

Mark Conner
June 2009

The Spirit of the LORD is upon me, for he has anointed me to bring good news to the poor. He has sent me to proclaim that captives will be released, that the blind will see, that the oppressed will be set free, and that the time of the LORD's favor has come.

Jesus (Luke 4:18-19)

INTRODUCTION

THE PRISONER

↑

Imagine a prison cell. There is a man lying on a cot with his back to the door. You hear footsteps approaching and the sound of a gate opening and closing. The prisoner doesn't move even when the footsteps stop at his cell. The following conversation then takes place.[1]

Joe: (not turning over) "Just drop them TJ . . . (Warden just stands there) . . . I don't have the energy to answer my door today."

Warden: "Mr. Rayburn . . . "

Joe: (rolls over) "Warden? TJ got you delivering magazines today?"

Warden: "No . . . but I am here with some news for you."

Joe: "News?"

---

1. This drama script was written by Donna Hinkle Lagerquist. Copyright © 1993 by Willow Creek Community Church. Used by permission.

Warden: ". . . from the Governor."

Joe: (rolling toward wall again) "Yeah, well, I don't want to hear about him refusing to hear my appeal again . . . I'd rather have my magazines." (yells) "Hey TJ?"

Warden: "I think you'll want to hear this news, Joe. The Governor has granted you clemency."

Joe: "What?"

Warden: "As of noon today, you are a free man."

Joe: (laughs) "Okay Warden, what's the catch? What's the joke . . . it's not very funny."

Warden: "It's no joke." (takes out papers) "Take a look for yourself, straight from the Governor's desk." (hands them to him)

Joe: (looks incredibly at papers) "What?"

Warden: "Read it for yourself."

Joe: "Why now . . . after 14 years?"

Warden: "Only the Governor can tell you that. I guess he never forgot your case."

Joe: "But I thought . . . "

Warden: "We contacted your sister. She's catching an afternoon flight and will be here this evening." (Warden takes out keys to unlock cell door)

Joe: "What are you doing?"

Warden: "I see no reason to keep this locked until noon. You're a free man, Joe. I'll finish up the paperwork as quickly as I can. Congratulations." (shakes Joe's hand after entering the cell and then exits)

Joe: (sits down in shock, reading) ". . . and that clemency has been granted to Mr. Joseph W. Rayburn." (pause) "I'm free? Just like that, I'm free?" (throws head back and howls)

"Whoa!" (stands, looks around and then yells) "Hey, TJ! I'm free!" (begins getting things together)

Imagine once again. The cell door is now open. Joe is sitting inside the cell playing solitaire. A janitor comes by the cell with a cleaning cart, singing. He turns to go into Joe's cell and is surprised to see him there.

Frank: "Joe? Man, I thought you'd have been long gone by now. What are you doing in there?"

Joe: "Playing the Solitaire Championship Playoff . . . and guess who's winning?"

Frank: "What?"

Joe: "I'm just playing some cards while I wait for my sister."

Frank: "In here?"

Joe: "What do you mean 'in here?' It's my cell, ain't it?"

Frank: "Not any more . . . they're putting a new guy in here tomorrow. You've been evicted, man. You're free."

Joe: "That's what the papers say." (gathers cards into pile)

Frank: "If I was you, I'd be outside. It's beautiful out there."

Joe: "Have you seen TJ?"

Frank: (not understanding) "Earlier this morning I did. Why?"

Joe: "He hasn't delivered my magazines. It's Thursday and it's after 2:00 pm. I should have my Newsweek by now."

Frank: "In case you didn't realize it, you don't need TJ to bring your magazines any more. You can go out and get your own Newsweek."

Joe: "Well, I'm sure TJ will be here any minute."

Frank: "What's the matter?" (as in "why aren't you leaving?")

Joe: (pause) "I don't know. It's just so sudden . . . I'm not ready."

Frank: "Not ready? To leave this hole? Are you nuts?"

Joe: "I've just gotten used to this . . . place."

Frank: "So? You saying you like it?"

Joe: "No, I'm not saying I like it . . . truth is, I hate it, but I know how to live here."

Frank: "But you live in a cell!"

Joe: "I know!" (frustrated and angry, slams door)

Frank: "Man, I can't figure you out." (exits)

Fast forward. It is evening now. Joe is doing sit-ups in his cell. His radio is on. The door is shut. We hear footsteps again, as Joe's sister approaches with an empty suitcase. She sets the suitcase down and watches him for a moment.

Linda: "Joey?"

Joe: (stops sit-ups and stands at door quickly) "Linda! Hi!"

Linda: "Hi. I brought this suitcase for all your things. It's brand new."

Joe: "I didn't hear you coming . . . have you been here long?"

Linda: "No . . . I'm here to bring you home . . . home! Can you believe it?"

Joe: (sits on cot) "No, no I can't."

Linda: "They told me they'd unlocked your cell." (looks at closed door) "I'll go get someone."

Joe: "It's unlocked, Linda."

Linda: (pause) "I talked to the Warden."

Joe: "He thinks I'm crazy, huh?"

Linda: "It'll just take some time, Joe. You'll get used to it."

Joe: "I'm not sure I want to go."

Linda: "Why?"

Joe: "I've been thinking . . . it's not so bad in here, Linda. I have everything I need. The food's not great but it's always there. And I can get things to read. I have a place to sleep."

Linda: "Joey, this is a prison!"

Joe: "And I am a prisoner!"

Linda: "No, you're not! The fact is . . . someone set you free."

Joe: "Free? Free for what?"

Linda: "To be whatever you've been robbed of being for the last fourteen years."

Joe: "I don't know."

Linda: "Joey, will you listen to yourself. How can you turn down fresh air and sunshine? How can you turn down life for . . . this? It doesn't make any sense!"

Joe: "I know it doesn't make any sense!"

Linda: "You won't be alone, Joey." (takes his hand) "Come on . . . let's just take a walk outside. Come on." (holds out hand to Joe) "We'll get your things later. Trust me, deep down inside you know this isn't how it's supposed to be."

Joe: (starts to leave, looks around) "I'm not sure . . . "

Linda: "Trust me, Joey. It's better out there."

Many of us have been like Joe at one time or another in our life. We've been in a prison. Maybe not a physical prison but possibly an emotional prison of worry, anger, fear, depression, rejection, addiction or spiritual bondage. Maybe you feel like you're in a prison right now.

The good news is that Jesus Christ has taken care of things for us and opened the door of our prison so that we can go free. That's the truth. The trouble is that sometimes a prison can become our home and moving out is not always as easy as it sounds. I pray that as you read through this book you will be encouraged to take some significant steps forward in your journey to find personal freedom in every area of your life . . . and then help others to do the same. Together let's make a prison break.

You will know the truth and the truth will set you free . . .
If the Son sets you free, you are truly free.

Jesus (John 8:32, 36)

The Lord is the Spirit and wherever the Spirit of the Lord
is, there is freedom.

The Apostle Paul (2 Corinthians 3:17)

Christ has truly set us free. Now make sure that you stay
free and don't get tied up again in the slavery of the law.

The Apostle Paul (Galatians 5:1)

CHAPTER ONE

PRISON BREAK

↑

As a young teenager I really struggled with insecurity. I had a lot of negative feelings about myself and I lacked personal confidence. I am not sure why. Possibly it was because I was a very tall, lanky redhead, who kind of stood out in any crowd. I was given many nicknames in those days. People called me "Big Red," "Carrot Top" or "Towering Inferno," just to mention a few.

I lived in America at the time but our family moved back to Australia where I completed Year 10 at Blackburn South High School in Melbourne. It was the 1970s and one of the most popular TV programs was *Happy Days*. Remember The Fonz? Back then I combed my hair on the side and when I arrived at school everyone started calling me "Ritchie," "Ritchie Cunningham," because I looked a lot like him. That didn't really help my identity crisis.

If a school teacher pointed me out in class and asked me to answer a question or read something out loud, my face would turn bright red as everyone stared at me. Even in the church youth group I attended, if I was asked to sing a solo for the choir, my face would be as red as my hair . . . through the whole song.

With all of this insecurity on the inside of me I would have never thought that I would one day lead a church and speak to thousands of people every weekend. Over a period of time God began to set me free. I was eventually able to come to a place where I realised that redheads are really cool, anyway. See, most people are burnt out. We are still on fire. I began to accept myself and come to a place of confidence where I really believed that God had something special for my life. I made a prison break from that prison of insecurity.

You may have a story of God helping you to break out of a prison. If you do, great. If not, then I believe that genuine freedom can become your experience too. Most of us have areas in our lives where we are somewhat bound up or locked up in a prison.

COMMON PRISONS

There are many things that can enslave us and keep us captive. Anger can take hold of our lives, as can bitterness. Fear can be a prison, as can lust and worry. Discouragement can also become a prison, where we feel so down over a failure or disappointment that it becomes hard to move on in life.

Grief is another thing that can bind people. Grief is a normal emotion that occurs anytime you lose something valuable. If you lose a job, a friend, a loved one, or an opportunity, then grief comes in. It takes time to work through these feelings of loss. However, if we are not careful, we can let that grief become a prison that keeps us captive to that loss and we never move on to what God has for us in the future.

Depression is another common thing that imprisons people. Depression has been referred to as the common cold of the emotions. Everyone has times when they have a low mood but sometimes that low mood can settle in and stay for an extended period. We feel hopeless and there is a sense of despair.

Bad habits can ensnare us. Habits that you try to break and then you slip back and then you try to break them again and you slip back. It is almost like a chain that holds you back. Bad habits can turn into addictions which can also be like a prison. We can be addicted to various activities or substances.

Alcohol is doing a lot of damage in our society today. It is really sad to see so many young people involved in binge drinking and the damage this does to their lives. No wonder the Bible has so many warnings about drunkenness and encourages us to either abstain from alcohol or, if we do drink, to drink in moderation.

Anything that controls us becomes like a prison that damages our lives. These are just a few of the things that can hold us captive, that can keep us in a prison and prevent us from experiencing the freedom that God has for us.

FREEDOM FOR THE PRISONERS

The good news is that Jesus came to free prisoners. He came to set captives free. Here is a record of one of Jesus' first sermons:

> Then Jesus returned to Galilee, filled with the Holy Spirit's power. Reports about him spread quickly through the whole region. He taught regularly in their synagogues and was praised by everyone.
>
> When he came to the village of Nazareth, his boyhood home, he went as usual to the synagogue on the Sabbath and stood up to read the Scriptures. The scroll of Isaiah the prophet was handed to him. He unrolled the scroll and found the place where this was written:
>
> "The Spirit of the LORD is upon me, for he has anointed me to bring Good News to the poor. He has sent me to proclaim that captives will be released, that the blind will see, that the oppressed will be set free, and that the time of the LORD's favor has come."
>
> He rolled up the scroll, handed it back to the attendant, and sat down. All eyes in the synagogue looked at him intently. Then he began to speak to them. "The Scripture you've just heard has been fulfilled this very day (Luke 4:14-21)!"

This is a very powerful story. Jesus had been in the wilderness for forty days. He had been fasting and he had overcome the temptations of the devil. He was now full of the Holy Spirit. In this sermon Jesus declared why he had come.

Part of his mission was to bring freedom to the prisoners. Jesus declared to any person who was in a prison of any kind that he had arrived to lead a prison break and to help them to be released from the captivity that the enemy had them in.

What great news it must have been to the people who heard Jesus preach that day. Jesus came to declare the heart of the Father God. All through the biblical story we see that God desired to set people free from anything that was trying to imprison them.

THE PRISON BREAKER

Let's go back to the story of Moses for a moment. Moses was minding his own business in a wilderness area when suddenly he saw a bush that was burning. He went over to see what was happening and God spoke to him out of that burning bush. This is what God said to Moses:

> I have certainly seen the oppression of my people in Egypt. I have heard their cries of distress because of their harsh slave drivers. Yes, I am aware of their suffering. So I have come down to rescue them from the power of the Egyptians and lead them out of Egypt into their own fertile and spacious land. It is a land flowing with milk and honey—the land where the Canaanites, Hittites, Amorites, Perizzites, Hivites, and Jebusites now live. Look! The cry of the people of Israel has reached me, and I have seen how harshly the Egyptians abuse them. Now go, for I am sending you to Pharaoh. You must lead my people Israel out of Egypt (Exodus 3:7-10).

God saw his people in Egypt and the terrible prison they were in. Not only did he see them, he heard them crying out. Not only did he hear them crying out, he was concerned about their suffering. He wanted to rescue them and he was sending Moses to deliver them.

God feels the same about us. If anything binds us, if we are in a prison, God sees it. He hears our cry. He is concerned about us. He wants to rescue us and send a prison break our way so that we can be free. That's good news. That's the heart of Father God for every one of us.

This theme of freedom flows right through the whole Bible. Jesus once said, "You will know the truth and the truth will set you free" and "If the Son sets you free, you are truly free (John 8:32, 36)." The apostle Paul said, "The Lord is the Spirit and wherever the Spirit of the Lord is, there is freedom (2 Corinthians 3:17)." Wherever God's Spirit turns up, there is freedom. People come out of captivity and bondage. They experience freedom in their life.

On another occasion Paul said, "Christ has truly set us free. Now make sure that you stay free and don't get tied up again in the slavery of the law (Galatians 5:1)." So it is very clear that God's will for our life is that we experience freedom, that we come out of any prison, that any chain that is holding us back be broken, and that we experience a prison break in our life.

THE FREEDOM PROCESS

How does that happen? How do you break out of a prison and out into the freedom that God has for you? Sometimes God works instantly. For example, salvation is an instant miracle. When you recognise that you need a saviour and you admit that you have done wrong, you ask God to forgive you and in an instant you are free from sin and condemnation. You are translated into the kingdom of God and you become his child. That is an incredible miracle that happens in an instant of time . . . even though it is usually a long journey up until that moment.

Maybe you have experienced that in your life. If you haven't, you are just a decision away from knowing that freedom which comes at salvation. However, you will find that most other instances of breaking free in our lives are usually not instant. There is often a process that takes a period of time. There is a journey that involves a number of steps.

As an illustration of this, think about Moses again. We know that it was the will of God to set his people free. However, Israel was not delivered from Egypt in an instant. It took time. There was a tug of war. Pharaoh did not want Israel to go. There were ten plagues. There was the temptation for Moses to compromise a number of times. The situation got worse before it got better. It was a long struggle before Israel escaped from Egypt and into the freedom that God had for them.

It was the same with Joshua. God gave Joshua a promise that everywhere he placed his foot God would give them the land. However, this didn't happen in a moment. No, it took a lot of time to move into the land and to defeat the many kings who were there. What was theirs legally had to become theirs in reality through possessing the land, step by step. It was a process for them to enter into the promises of God.

It is the same with the Christian life. Even though salvation occurs in an instant and one day when Jesus comes back we will be glorified in an instant and sin will be eradicated from our lives, in between there is this process called "sanctification." Have you noticed that this does not happen in an instant? It takes a life time to become like Jesus, to put off old habits and to put on new habits.

This is the way God set up the world. Every aspect of life involves a process of change. Consider agriculture as an example. If you want to eat an apple for lunch today you can't go into your backyard and look for an apple if you haven't planted an apple tree and nurtured it. The apple is not going to be there. If you want to reap the apple, you have to plant the apple seed, let it die, then nurture it through the seasons. You have to sow before you reap. If you buy an apple at the grocery store today, you are only doing so because someone else did all that work for you. You have to go through the process. There is no such thing as an instant apple.

If you are married and you decide you want to have children, the baby is not going to be there tomorrow. There is a nine month process to go through that includes morning sickness, kicking, stretching, and pain (which every mother knows about). Then eventually, with the dad cheering on, the baby arrives. You can have the dream and the plan and all the aspirations, but you can't avoid the process.

It is the same with habits. You might decide today to start a new habit. However, psychologists tell us that it takes about twenty-one days to establish a new habit until it is automatic in your life. Years ago, when I was involved in music, I had a friend who had played the flute for many years. She went to a new teacher who was an outstanding flute player and she discovered that the way she was holding her mouth, her embouchure, was wrong. So, at her first flute lesson, she was taught the proper way to position her mouth on the flute. Did she change the next day? No, it took many months for her to unlearn the way she had played for many years and to develop a new habit.

Think of a caterpillar. It wants to become a butterfly. This doesn't happen by it singing the hit song, "I believe I can fly. I believe I can touch the sky" by R. Kelly. No, the caterpillar has to go into a cocoon. There will be some darkness and there will be some struggle but over time a butterfly will emerge. If you're like me, you wish God would eliminate this middle stuff. It can be frustrating and annoying. I would rather simply experience a quick zap and have the freedom come in an instant but I have come to understand that God has a purpose in the process.

It seems that God is more interested in our character than our comfort. That is because it is in the process that we grow, we mature, and we change. If you break open a cocoon and try to help the caterpillar along, you will destroy the beautiful butterfly that God is in the process of making.

Yes, God wants freedom in every area of our life. However, moving towards freedom, more often than not, involves a process that takes time. It is not always easy. We need to be careful that we don't become discouraged and give up on our faith along the way.

THE FREEDOM PARTNERSHIP

Freedom is also a partnership between God and us. It is God's work and it is our work. We need to balance these two aspects. If we only rely on God, we can sit in our prison and wait for God to free us. That's probably not going to happen. Or we can take it all on ourselves and try to find our own freedom. Without God's power we will probably never be free. It is God and us working together. The apostle Paul put it this way:

> Therefore, my dear friends, as you have always obeyed, not only in my presence but now much more in my absence, continue to *work out* your salvation with fear and trembling, for it is God who *works in* you to will and to act according to His good purpose (Philippians 2:12-13. NIV).

This is how God works in our lives. He works in us by his spirit. He is the one who opens the prison door. He has the power to break chains. Without him working in us we are never going to be free but we have to work things out too. We have to walk out of our prison. We have to take some steps and co-operate with God in order to enter into the freedom that he has for us.

FIRST MOVEMENT: FROM DENIAL TO CONFESSION

There are five movements that we need to make in order to co-operate with God so that we can break out of any prison that may be holding us captive. The first movement is from denial to confession. If we deny that we are even in a prison, we will never be free.

Alcoholics Anonymous has been helping people find freedom from alcohol addiction for many decades now and they make use of twelve steps. The first step when people join a group is that they have to admit that they are an alcoholic. This is because if a person denies that they even have a problem they will never be free. Freedom starts with moving out of denial into confessing that we need help. That can be pretty humbling. However, it is a required step for finding personal freedom.

SECOND MOVEMENT: FROM EXCUSES TO RESPONSIBILITY

The second movement is from excuses to responsibility. The apostle Paul says this:

> When I was a child, I spoke and thought and reasoned as a child. But when I grew up, I put away childish things (1 Corinthians 13:11).

One common childish tendency is to make excuses. We are quick to blame others rather than take responsibility for our life. Sometimes, when we are in a prison, instead of taking responsibility to break out of that prison, we blame other people for putting us in the prison.

People in a prison of bitterness find it is easy to talk about the people who have hurt them and what has been done to them as a justification for their situation. However, although other people do influence the prisons that we can end up in, we are responsible for how we respond to what they have done and to what we are going to do in response. If we stay in the land of excuses, we will never be free. We have to move from excuses to taking responsibility.

You may be in a prison. Maybe others have contributed to that but it is now your responsibility to decide whether you are going to stay in that prison or whether you are going to seek to break out of it. We need to move towards personal responsibility.

THIRD MOVEMENT: FROM INDEPENDENCE TO COMMUNITY

The third movement is from independence towards community. This is a difficult one. We live in a world where self-help is so popular. Walk into any bookshop and you will find an entire section of resources on topics such as three ways to build your self esteem or six ways to improve your sex life. The focus is on how you, by yourself, can fix your life. There is some merit in this but I have discovered that a lot of the freedom and the change that God wants to bring about in our lives, we will not be able to achieve by ourselves. We need people to assist us in becoming free.

Listen to what James says about this:

Confess your sins to each other and pray for each other so that you may be healed (James 5:16).

This sounds somewhat uncomfortable. In fact, the way we often live our lives is probably the opposite of this instruction. We tend to not want to tell anyone that we have faults. We try to work on them by ourselves so no-one will ever know we had a problem.

In contrast, James says that if we are in a prison, if we are struggling, or if we have a fault we should confess it to some friends, some brothers and sisters in Christ, and have them pray for us. He then says that the prayer of those in relationship with us will be part of our healing and release. That is why we need to be closely connected with other people.

Part of our freedom may involve sharing with some trusted friends about an area that we are struggling with and asking them to pray for us. There is something powerful that happens when others join with us to help us break through to freedom. Other people can provide support for us, encouragement, feedback, accountability, as well as wise counsel.

Maybe you are in a prison of depression that has been lingering for a long time. One component of your journey to freedom may involve going and speaking to a mature Christian or a qualified counsellor and asking for their help. Often we need other people to help us out of our prison.

FOURTH MOVEMENT: FROM COMPLACENCY TO DESPERATION

The fourth movement is from complacency towards desperation. Do we really want to be free? One day a blind man came up to Jesus and Jesus said, "What do you want me to do for you (Mark 10:51)?" This seems quite unusual. The man was blind yet Jesus did not assume that the blind man really wanted to see.

Sometimes we become comfortable in our prison. Our prison can become our home. It becomes our security. In fact, it can define who we are. If we are going to be free, we have to move from the comfort and complacency of what has been binding us and come to a place of desperation where we really want to change . . . whatever it takes.

FIFTH MOVEMENT: FROM LETHARGY TO VIGILANCE

The fifth and final movement is from lethargy to vigilance. We are in a spiritual battle. Not only does God want freedom in our lives, the enemy wants to keep us captive. That is why we have to be regularly on guard, vigilant and watchful so we don't fall back into the captivity that we have been set free from. Every one of us is only one decision away from a major disaster in our life. We must not become lethargic. We need to be spiritually awake and alert so that we keep the freedom God has for each one of us.

IT'S YOUR MOVE

God wants a prison break in every one of our lives. He wants us free from any prison that the enemy may be holding us in. This happens through a process of time. It is a partnership between God and us. He has opened the prison door. It's our choice now as to whether to move out or not.

We need to be willing to move from denial into a place where we confess that we need help. We need to move from making excuses and blaming other people into a place of taking personal responsibility for our lives. We need to move from trying to do it all by ourselves to recognising that we need other people to help us. We have to move from complacency into desperation. We need to really want to change. Finally, we need to move from lethargy to vigilance, where we are constantly on guard in order to protect our freedom.

Is God highlighting an area or an issue in your life right now? It might be one of the areas I have mentioned in this first chapter. It could be insecurity, like I went through. It could be anger. It could be bitterness. It could be a habit. It could be an addiction. It could be worry. It could be any area. What do you need freedom from? I pray that you will experience a prison break beginning today.

DISCLAIMER

My intention for this book is not for it to be a quick-fix, self-help guide. I have discovered that God doesn't operate by formulas. We shouldn't buy into the idea that, "If you do A, B, and C, then D will always happen." Life is not always black and white either. There are a lot more grey areas than we'd prefer to admit. God rarely works in the same way in every circumstance. Each person is unique as is each situation. There are always exceptions to every rule. Life is complex.

However, I have discovered that there are general principles for life that God has established that can be of benefit to each one of us. In this book, I will share some of those principles. They have helped me in my personal life and other people have also found them beneficial. My prayer is that you will find them helpful too.

PRAYER

If you have never surrendered your life to Jesus Christ, then I encourage you to say the following prayer out loud.

"Dear heavenly Father, thank you for loving me so much that you sent Jesus to die for my sin. Please forgive me for everything I have done wrong. Make me your child. Fill me with your Spirit. I will live for you. I will serve you all the days of my life and when my life is over I know I will spend eternity with you, in Jesus name, Amen."

Let me pray for you now.

"Father, I pray for those who said that prayer from their heart. You said that if we confess you as the Lord of our life and believe it in our heart we will be saved. Come inside of them right now. Fill them with your Spirit. Make them your child. Give them an assurance of their salvation. Wash away all of the pain, guilt and shame of the past. Let today be a new day of walking with you and living for you. Show them your purpose for their life, in Jesus' name. Amen."

"Father, I also pray that you will enable us to make a prison break in every area of our life. May we find the freedom that you have made available to us. Freedom is our heritage. It's why Jesus came. Hear our cry. Break chains and open prison doors. Help us to step out of that prison door. Set us free today, I pray. May there be a breakthrough in our lives so that over the days and weeks to come we will move into full freedom. We will be sure to give you the praise and honour and glory, in Jesus' name, Amen."

REFLECTION QUESTIONS

1. Read Luke 4:14-21. What does this tell us about Jesus and his ministry?

2. Read Exodus 3:7-10. What does this tell us about God's heart for us as his people?

3. What area(s) of freedom has God helped you to experience? How did change come about? Was it instantaneous or did it take place over a period of time?

4. What area would you like to experience freedom in right now? Pray and ask God about it now. Consider telling a safe friend. I pray that as you continue to read this book, you will experience a time of God's favour in your life and that the Holy Spirit will give you the power to break free from whatever may be holding you in a prison.

5. The ultimate freedom in life is freedom from guilt and sin. Pray for someone you know who does not know God yet. Pray for their salvation and freedom.

CHAPTER TWO

FREEDOM FROM WORRY

↑

The year 2008 started in a horrific way for our family. The phone on my bedside table startled me as it started ringing at 5.30 a.m. on New Year's day. I found the phone and answered it, still half asleep. I didn't recognise the man's voice on the other end but he proceeded to ask me if we had a son named Josiah. The message was that Josiah had just been in a serious car accident and that we needed to get to the scene as soon as possible. After scribbling down the address as quick as I could, Nicole and I jumped out of bed, threw some clothes on, and sped off in our car. The drive to the address that the unknown caller had given me took about thirty minutes but it seemed like an eternity. Talk about worry. Our minds were racing with all sorts of questions about what had happened, who was involved, and whether they would be alright or not.

After working through the stress and frustration of getting lost by taking a wrong turn along the way, we finally arrived at the intersection where the accident had recently taken place. There were ambulances everywhere. Our three children and two of their friends were travelling in a car that collided head on into another vehicle. Both vehicles were smashed beyond repair.

We were very grateful that all five of them were still alive, after what could have been a fatal accident. There is no doubt that the prayers of God's people and some vigilant guardian angels made the difference. One of the policemen attending the scene told me that from his experience only one in a million people walk away from an accident this serious.

Very late on that first day of the year , Nicole and I finally crept into bed but with none of our children at home with us. They were all in the hospital emergency ward, along with their friends. Those next few days and weeks were difficult ones. God gave me some thoughts from the Bible that encouraged all of us during this time:

I will never forget this awful time, as I grieve over my loss. Yet I still dare to hope when I remember this: The faithful love of the Lord never ends! His mercies never cease. Great is his faithfulness; his mercies begin afresh each morning. I say to myself, "The Lord is my inheritance; therefore, I will hope in him (Lamentations 3:20-24)!"

At times thoughts drifted into thinking about what could have happened and how I would have handled a more serious outcome. However, it was too emotional for me to go there with my mind. I was very aware that this good news survival story was not everyone's testimony. We have some friends who are pastors, whose adult son was killed in a motorbike accident just a few days before this accident, leaving his wife and two young children. Our hearts broke for them and we prayed for their comfort during their time of intense grief.

Our children and their friends gradually recovered from their injuries - broken bones, stitches, scratches and bruises. All of us as parents spent plenty of time worrying during this time as to whether they'd all be okay or not. It was not an easy time. Nevertheless, God's grace was strong and the prayers and support of our family, friends and church community were so appreciated.

When anyone experiences a traumatic time such as this, worry can really take a grip of your life. I had a much less serious experience with worry when I was in my twenties. At that time, I had been given the responsibility of overseeing the worship ministry of the church I attended. This involved leading singing, playing the piano, and organising various special events. I really enjoyed this season of my life.

Around this time I received a call from Integrity Music in the USA. They were about to do a tour around the major cities of Australia with a worship leader named Ron Kenoly. It was the *Lift Him Up* tour and they asked if I would play keyboards as part of the band. I was really excited at such a great opportunity to work with Ron and the team, and to travel around the country together. So I agreed to accept their offer.

Over the next few months, I experienced a great deal of nervous excitement on the inside of me and a fair amount of worry too. Many of the songs we would be playing were fairly complex. I would be part of a band of mainly professional musicians who had played for many years, including on studio albums. I had played piano at church meetings and conferences, as well as a small amount of studio work, but not at their level of expertise. I started practising a lot but I was worried that I wouldn't be able to play at their level.

Funnily enough, I had some really crazy dreams leading up to this particular tour. I remember one night dreaming that I had arrived at this large auditorium filled with thousands of people and the meeting was about to start. I was standing in front of the keyboards and then I looked down and I was still in my underwear! People were staring at me and laughing. I was freaking out. Then I suddenly woke up thanking God that it was only a dream.

A few weeks later I had another similar dream. The worship event had already started. I was in my car and I was late. I could not get through the heavy traffic. Everyone in the band was there playing except for me. There was no keyboard player. Then I woke up and realised that it was just a dream. Worry was taking a hold of my life during this time.

WHAT A WORRY WORRY IS!

What about you? Do you ever worry? Maybe the better question is, "What do you worry about?" We all worry from time to time. Maybe you have an exam coming up and you are worrying about whether you are going to pass or fail it. You might have an interview this week and you are hoping that they offer you the job. Maybe you have recently become a small group leader and you are a little nervous about whether anyone is going to turn up.

Finances are another area that we worry about. Will we have enough money to pay the bills or how are we going to work through this mountain of debt? We can worry about our health. If we are well, we worry that we might get sick. If we are sick, we worry about whether we'll ever get well again.

We can worry about relationships. If you are single and you would like to be married you can worry if you will ever meet the right person. If you are married you can worry if you married the right person. Maybe you are having some intense arguments at the moment and that is worrying you. Maybe you have children and you worry about them when they are not with you, that something bad might happen. If you have teenagers you might be worrying about where they are, who they are with, and what they are doing or maybe you are worried about your parents.

In addition to our own lives and personal relationships there is also the world around us which can be a cause of worry. We worry about the economy and the increasing price of fuel. Home mortgages are becoming bigger and house prices are increasing. Then there is the threat of terrorism. There is the problem of global warning.

There are many things to worry about that are real and relevant to our lives. When we worry we begin to fret and we become anxious. We become overly concerned. Worry is simply negative meditation or negative imagination.

One worry feeds another so much that it becomes impossible to think of anything other than the risks and the threats that could lie ahead. The more we worry, the worse we feel; the worse we feel, the more we think in a worried and anxious way. We can lose our joy worrying about circumstances that may never happen, or that turn out to be not as bad as we had imagined, or we worry about matters that were never that important to begin with. Worry rarely helps.

DON'T WORRY!

Once again, as we turn to God's Word as recorded in the Bible, we find some really good advice and encouragement for finding freedom from worry. Jesus spoke about worry in his sermon on the mountain. He wants to set us free from worry so that our minds are not preoccupied with the cares and concerns of life. Here is what he said.

> That is why I tell you not to worry about everyday life— whether you have enough food and drink, or enough clothes to wear. Isn't life more than food, and your body more than clothing (Matthew 6:25)?

In that culture there were a few wealthy people but many of the people Jesus ministered to were peasants. Even basic needs were often hard to come by. Many people were worried about their next meal or having enough clothing for the cold winter. Jesus continued.

> Look at the birds. They don't plant or harvest or store food in barns, for your heavenly Father feeds them. And aren't you far more valuable to him than they are? Can all your worries add a single moment to your life?

And why worry about your clothing? Look at the lilies of the field and how they grow. They don't work or make their clothing, yet Solomon in all his glory was not dressed as beautifully as they are. And if God cares so wonderfully for wildflowers that are here today and thrown into the fire tomorrow, he will certainly care for you. Why do you have so little faith?

So don't worry about these things, saying, "What will we eat? What will we drink? What will we wear?" These things dominate the thoughts of unbelievers, but your heavenly Father already knows all your needs. Seek the kingdom of God above all else, and live righteously, and he will give you everything you need.

So don't worry about tomorrow, for tomorrow will bring its own worries. Today's trouble is enough for today (Matthew 6:26-34).

Multiple times Jesus said, "Don't worry!" He told people not to allow their mind and heart to become a prisoner to worry. In another teaching, Jesus told a parable of a sower who was sowing seeds in different types of soil. There was the good soil, the soil with the stones in it, as well as soil with thorns in it. Jesus interpreted the parable by saying that the worries of this life can become like thorns which choke and strangle the life out of God's word, causing us to be unfruitful (Matthew 13:22).

In this story, thorns are a metaphor for worry. Worry chokes the joy out of life. That is why Jesus told people to not allow themselves to become caught up with worry. He wanted them to remove worry from their life so that it didn't become a prison around them.

How can we stop worrying? There are four actions that we can take to break free from a prison of worry.

SPECIFY YOUR WORRIES

First of all, we need to specify our worries. Worry can be like a vague, nebulous cloud hanging around filling us with thoughts of all the bad things that could or might happen. Find a piece of paper and write down a list of everything you are worried about. When you move your worries out of your head and on to some paper they become more specific. You can then deal with them more easily.

A study was done a number of years ago looking into the issues that people worry about. The conclusion of the research was that forty percent of things that we tend to worry about are never going to happen. They are totally improbable. They are not going to take place. Many people's lives are filled with tragedies that never actually happen.

Thirty percent of what people worry about is in the past. It has already taken place. It is over and done with. They can't do anything about it but people still worry.

Ten percent of what people worry about is menial. It is trivial. It is so small that it is not a big deal.

Twelve percent of people's worries are related to their health. Interestingly enough, worrying makes your health worse. So we are up to ninety-two percent.

The final eight percent of people's worries are about things that are legitimate. They are real, tangible worries. However, only half (or four percent) of these are things that people can do something about. The other four percent are matters beyond a person's control.

Research reveals that ninety-six percent of what we worry about is not worth worrying about. What a worry, worry is. No wonder Jesus says, "Don't worry!"

The very process of specifying our worries helps us to analyse our worries as to their legitimacy. You will probably see matters that you are worrying about that are not going to happen, that are improbable, that are in your past and that are menial. You can then eliminate those worries that are not worth worrying about. This is the first step to breaking free from worry.

TAKE ACTION ON YOUR WORRIES

The next step is to take action on your worries. Look at your legitimate worries and ask whether you can do anything about them. If you can, then turn each worry into an action. Turn it into a problem and begin solving the problem. When we begin taking action on our worry we begin to change the situation and worry begins to disappear. This is very simple but it is very powerful.

For example, let's say that you are driving home from work. As you are driving, a red light starts to flash on your dashboard indicating that your fuel tank is on empty. You can either start worrying and thinking about the possibility of running out of petrol and having to walk home or you can turn that worry into an action.

Worry can become your friend in this case. It is grabbing your attention about an important matter. Stop and fill up with fuel and then that red light will go away without you having to smash it. You can then keep driving home and your worry will have disappeared. You have turned your worry into an action.

Let me give you another example. Maybe you have lots of pot plants at home. You walk by one and it is dying. You can start worrying about the possibility of it dying and how sad that would be or you can turn that worry into an action. Go ahead and water the plant. It will start to grow again and the worry will be gone.

If you are a small group leader, let's say that you have not seen Mary for three weeks and so you start worrying about her. You wonder whether she is alright, whether she is away from God or maybe she was hit by a car. You can spend days and even weeks wondering and worrying about whether Mary is okay or not. Rather than do that, turn that worry into an action. Get on the phone and call her. Tell her you haven't seen her for a while and you were wondering if everything is alright. She has probably been on holidays.

Sometimes we waste a lot of time and energy on things we keep worrying about. If we would turn each worry into an action, we would find that things tend to work out alright. They are often not worth worrying about.

Has someone been a bit cool to you lately? You can start worrying that you may have offended them. If your mind goes down this worry track you start to think that maybe they don't like you anymore. You can blow the entire situation out of proportion and it will become bigger than Ben Hur. If you would just give them a call and ask them if everything is alright between you, you might find out that they are working through another issue in their life and it has nothing to do with you at all.

OFFER A PRAYER TO GOD

The third step to breaking free from worry is to offer up a prayer to God. The apostle Paul picks up the teaching of Jesus and he gives us some additional insight on how to stop worrying. Here is what he said in a letter to some believers living in the city of Philippi.

> Do not be anxious about anything, but in everything, by prayer and petition, with thanksgiving, present your requests to God. And the peace of God, which transcends all understanding, will guard your hearts and your minds in Christ Jesus (Philippians 4:6-7).

Like Jesus, Paul tells us not to worry. He also gives us a suggestion as to how to do this. He tells us to bring every worry to God in prayer. The Message Bible translates Paul's comments this way:

> Don't fret or worry. Instead of worrying, pray. Let petitions and praises shape your worries into prayers, letting God know your concerns. Before you know it, a sense of God's wholeness, everything coming together for good, will come and settle you down. It's wonderful what happens when

Christ displaces worry at the centre of your life (Philippians 4:6-7).

I love that. Shape your worries into prayers letting God know your concerns. It is a great idea to use worry as a motivator for prayer. If you find yourself starting to worry about your teenager, use your worry as a trigger to start praying for them. Bring them before God and pray for God's blessing and protection over their life. Turn all worry into a prayer. Turn the negative into a positive.

What the enemy sent to become a prison for you, you turn it around. Begin to pray God's will into that area. What a difference it would make in our world if every time we began to worry we simply shaped that worry into a prayer aimed at impacting the situation positively. Worry accomplishes nothing yet prayer has tremendous power. If we shape our worries into prayer, instead of allowing worry to be at the centre of our life, God's peace comes in. Christ comes in and we are freed from that prison of worry.

PLACE YOUR TRUST IN GOD

The final step is to place your trust in God. This is especially important for those worries that we can do nothing about. There is no action we can take on these worries so we choose to place our trust in God.

When Jesus taught about worry he used birds as an example. Birds trust their heavenly Father to feed them. Yes, they are busy. They are not sitting around waiting for food.

They are doing what they can but ultimately their Father is the one providing for them.

You and I need to realise that in our life there will be uncertainties and matters beyond our control. There will be contradictions and there will be times when we do not know what to do. There is no action we can take. However, the good news is that our life is not subject to fate, luck or chance. Our life is under the sovereign control of God. Nothing comes our way without him being aware of it and allowing it.

We need to trust in God and his providence. He is working all things together for our benefit. Here is what the apostle Paul had to say about this:

> And we know that God causes everything to work together for the good of those who love God and are called according to his purpose for them (Romans 8:28-29).

Notice that it does not say that all things are good. There are things that come our way that are not good. Bad things do happen to good people. It does not say that all things have a happy ending or that all things work out the way we want them to. It also does not say that God causes all things. God does not cause war or terrorism or rape. There are a lot of things that God does not directly cause.

What it does say is that God causes everything – the good, the bad, and the ugly – to work together for our ultimate benefit when we love him. That requires trust because we do not always understand how that is going to happen. We cannot figure it all out but if we place our trust in God it will help us to break free from a prison of worry.

Here is a well-known proverb that has a lot of wisdom about this area of trust. It is a wonderful promise.

Trust in the Lord with all your heart and lean not on your own understanding; in all your ways acknowledge him, and he will make your paths straight (Proverbs 3:5-6).

With the promise comes a premise or a condition to the promise being fulfilled. We are to trust, which means to put our faith and our confidence in God. We are not to lean or rely on our own understanding or wisdom and we are to acknowledge our need for God in our life. If we obey these three instructions, there is a promise that God will make our paths straight.

The Hebrew word for "straight" has the idea of someone going ahead and clearing the path, making it smooth and providing guidance for where we need to go. I am sure that you want God to make your paths straight. I sure do, because I do not see my whole journey. I am not sure what the next turn is or what is up ahead but I have a God who sees the future. I want him making my paths straight so that I do not trip up or get lost.

DON'T LOSE YOUR JOY

Some of you may be wondering about the Ron Kenoly tour. Did I turn up in my underwear? No. I knew specifically what I was worrying about. I took action. I practised really hard and I prepared well. I knew that God did not open this door of opportunity for me to fail or to make a fool of myself. I placed my trust in him and it went fine. We had a great tour and some very powerful worship times together.

God can help you to be free from your worry. He can even use it as a catalyst to bring you into the life that he has for you. Worry is a waste of time and energy. Worry takes away your joy. In fact, it is impossible to worry and be joyful at the same time. That is why the apostle Paul tells us to rejoice in the Lord at all times (Philippians 4:4). He does not say that we should worry at all times because when worry comes in, joy disappears.

God wants us to live a life of joy. That does not mean that all the circumstances will necessarily be in our favour. When Paul wrote that statement, he was in prison. There were limitations in his world and yet he was able to rejoice. He refused to let worry establish itself in his heart and life.

One last thought about worry. The subtle thing about worry is that it causes us to become preoccupied with our own needs. So much so, that we miss out on the needs and opportunities of those around about us. In Jesus' teaching on worry which we referred to earlier, he gave us a key to conquer worry. After saying multiple times that people should not worry, he said that instead of worrying we should seek first the kingdom of God (Matthew 6:33). In other words, Jesus said that the antidote to worry is to be busy focusing on what God is doing, on advancing his kingdom, on looking for needs around us and using our gifts to make a difference in the world.

When we become busy helping to meet the needs of other people, it is somewhat of a paradox. God comes along and he helps us with all of our own concerns, all those things that we are legitimately worried about. He brings all of his resources to bear because we are now not preoccupied with them. We are focused on advancing his kingdom.

Don't allow worry to become like a prison that saps you of your joy, drains you of your energy and causes you to get caught up with your own needs. If you do, you will miss out on many opportunities to be a blessing. The greatest level of living is not to be blessed. It is to be a blessing and to make a difference in the lives of other people. I pray today that if there is anything that you have been worrying about that some of the principles we have shared from God's Word will help you to break free from worry.

PRAYER

Here is my prayer for you:

"Father, we thank you for the joy of the gospel, that there is freedom for the prisoners. All of us have known what it's like to be in a prison of worry. I thank you that there is freedom from worry.

I pray for those reading this book right now that you would free them from any and every worry that may have taken a grip on their life. Help them to let go of the many things that are not worth worrying about. For the genuine concerns that they have, I ask that you would come alongside them and help them to take action where they can. Where they cannot take action, I pray that they would be able to trust you.

Help them to place all of their worries in a box and hand them to you, knowing that you care for them. You are interested in their world and their life. Lord, as they trust in you, you are going to make their paths straight. Free them from worry right now. Break open that prison door. Even in the midst of a storm, may they know your peace in their heart. May they know your joy. You are in control. Give them your abundant grace which is always more than enough for all that we go through, in Jesus' name. Amen."

REFLECTION QUESTIONS

1. Reflect back on your life and consider various situations in which you spent considerable time worrying. What happened? Was the worry worth it? How did each circumstance turn out?

2. Read Matthew 6:25-34 where Jesus taught on worry. If Jesus were speaking this today, what would be some of the common worries he might have mentioned?

3. Reflect on how taking positive action helps conquer worry. Think about how prayer can assist us in conquering worry. Take a moment right now to pray about each one of your worries.

4. Reflect on the concept of "trust" in God. How does this help conquer worry? Read Proverbs 3:5-6. What is the promise? What are the three conditions to the promise?

CHAPTER THREE

FREEDOM FROM ANGER

↑

Back in the first century, the apostle James wrote a letter to some followers of Christ to offer them some practical advice for living the kind of life God desired for them. He was particularly interested in the quality of their relationships. Here is what he said.

> Understand this, my dear brothers and sisters: You must all be quick to listen, slow to speak, and slow to get angry. Human anger does not produce the righteousness God desires (James 1:19-21).

James shares three important keys to great relationships. First of all, we need to become good listeners. Second, we have to think before we open our mouth and speak. Third, we need to learn to control our anger. I am sure that you would agree with James that anger can do a lot of damage in our relationships if we are not careful.

Human relationships are an essential part of all of our lives. They are where we experience some of our greatest joys. They are also where we sometimes experience our deepest pain. Some of that pain can be caused by uncontrolled anger. In this chapter we want to discuss how we can be free from a prison of destructive anger.

ANGER IS A COMMON EMOTION

Let's begin by making a few general observations about anger. First of all, we need to recognise that anger is a common emotion. Even James acknowledges that anger is a potential threat to every relationship. Every person experiences times when they feel annoyed, irritated, resentful and angry. Adults feel angry. Children feel angry. Young people, old people, employers, employees, parents and yes, even pastors. Everyone feels anger at various times in their life.

Individual people express their feelings of anger in different ways. Some people withdraw when they are angry. Other people let out a verbal, heated barrage of words. Others withhold affection. Some people may even become so angry and aggressive that they become physically violent. Murder is an example of extreme anger.

The Bible makes frequent reference to the problem of anger. It needs to be handled correctly. We are told about the dangers of uncontrolled anger and the benefits of being a person who is slow to become angry.

Anger can come from the frustration of having our goal blocked. For instance, the driver in front of us is going ten kilometres slower than the speed limit and we are in a real hurry. Or someone is an hour late for that appointment that we made an extra effort to be on time for. Or that referee just made a stupid call. Frustration causes anger. Hurt from the words or actions of other people can also stir up anger inside of us.

Anger, like most of our emotions, is a warning signal that some sort of violation has taken place. We need to pay attention to it. However, we need to choose wisely what we do in response to our feelings of anger.

ANGER CAN CAUSE GREAT DAMAGE

The second observation about anger is that it can cause great damage. James makes this very clear. He says, "Human anger does not produce the righteousness God desires." Anger is a major destroyer of relationships and it has been causing damage to relationships for a long time.

The very first family conflict was between two brothers. Cain became so angry that he ended up killing his brother Abel (Genesis 4:1-16). Not a lot has changed throughout the centuries. Browse through your local newspaper and you will see the evidence of anger throughout many of the stories, whether it is a war taking place in another country, an angry union strike, a celebrity going through a nasty divorce settlement or an assault charge because of someone expressing their anger in a violent manner. Anger is everywhere and it causes a lot of damage.

Christian family counsellor Gary Smalley tells us that anger creates distance between us and the person that we are angry with. There is often a withdrawal of some kind. There is no desire to interact or be close. Anger also creates darkness. The apostle John tells us that when we hate someone we are in darkness (1 John 2:9-11). When there is anger in a relationship, darkness comes in and we lose perspective. We cannot think logically and we stumble around.

Another thing that anger does is that it ties us up in knots. In the inner part of our world, our spirit and our emotions become all tied up. That is why forgiveness is so important. Forgiveness is the only thing that unties those knots. The word "forgive" literally means to let go, to untie or to unbind.

Anger is so destructive that it also hurts the person who is angry. It is like a boomerang. We become angry at someone else but our anger affects us too. No wonder the book of Proverbs warns us so frequently about anger. Proverbs 14:17 says that short-tempered people do foolish things. Proverbs 29:22 says that an angry person starts fights and a hot-tempered person commits all kinds of sin. When anger enters any relationship it can do terrible damage.

ANGER MANAGEMENT IS ESSENTIAL

The third observation about anger is that anger management is essential for healthy relationships. It is vital that you and I bring our anger under control. This is not an easy task but it is something that we need to focus our energy on. A lot of people will tolerate other emotional dysfunctions. We may struggle with shyness or insecurity. However, anger is such a potentially damaging emotion that it is very important that we learn to manage and control it.

For those of us who are leaders or in a position of authority, it is vital that we learn to manage our anger because we represent God to people. Anger does a lot of damage when it comes from an authority figure. In fact, even secular studies on leadership today say that the best leaders have what could be called a "non-anxious presence." That is, they remain calm in all situations and that emotional state positively impacts their followers. It is so important that we take control of this emotion of anger and ensure that it does not destroy people around about us.

DISTINGUISHING BETWEEN FEELINGS AND BEHAVIOUR

The fourth observation about anger is that there is a big difference between having angry feelings and expressing angry behaviour. The apostle Paul says, "In your anger, do not sin (Ephesians 4:26)." The Good News translation says, "If you become angry, do not let your anger lead you into sin." How can we be angry and not sin? We do this by distinguishing between feelings of anger and angry behaviour.

The emotion of anger is not the problem. It is what we do with our angry feelings. If you are angry, and all of us will be at some time, it is important that we make sure that we manage those feelings of anger in a constructive Christ-like manner. Where the sin comes in is when we take those angry feelings and translate them into behaviour that damages other people.

There is nothing wrong with the angry feeling itself. Believing that you should never get angry can be an unrealistic expectation that we place on ourselves. It is one thing to feel angry. It is yet another thing to then vent that anger through behaviour that hurts people.

UNDERSTANDING RIGHTEOUS ANGER

There is a place for righteous anger. God expresses anger at times. However, his anger is a lot different than ours. God's anger is never irrational or as a result of impatience. The Bible describes God as being "not easily angered" (Exodus 34:6). When God is angry his anger only lasts for a moment and it is always an expression of his goodness and concern. This does not mean that God's anger is not serious. However, when God is angry, it is always for our good and so that we will return to him.

We also, at times, should be moved to a sense of righteous anger. God seeks to stir us about things that offend him and that damage people. One of the criticisms of western Christianity is that we have lost our sense of outrage. It is so easy for us to become so focused on being balanced and tolerant and politically correct and even relevant, that we can end up sticking our head in the sand and remaining silent about the injustices of our world. It is so easy to become angry about things that really do not matter and to be indifferent about the things that really do. There are many injustices taking place in our generation that should arouse righteous anger that motivates us to do something about seeing them change.

In summary, anger is a common emotion. We all feel it. Anger can cause great damage. We need to learn to manage it if we want healthy relationships. There is a big difference between angry feelings and behaviour and there is an appropriate place for righteous anger.

YOUR ANGER TRIGGERS

How do we take control of our anger? The first action that I have found helpful is to think about what we could call "anger triggers." Look at your life and your relationships and consider what causes you to become angry. What kind of people tend to make you angry? What are some of the situations where anger is most aroused in you?

If you do not take the time to evaluate your anger triggers, you will find that you will establish cycles or habit patterns where circumstances happen and you become angry without even thinking. Stop, reflect, and analyse the situations that stir anger within you. By doing so, you will learn and grow.

A common anger trigger is people. Certain people, with their personality traits, idiosyncrasies and quirks, are an ever present source of potential irritation. If there were no other people in the world we would probably have a lot less anger.

The external environment can also be an anger trigger. It could be a simple inconvenience, a difficult circumstance, a flat tyre, or rain on a day when you planned your barbecue. These types of events happen and they can trigger angry feelings inside of us. We can also be our own anger trigger. Our own weaknesses, inadequacies and failures can stir up anger within us.

By reflecting on our anger triggers we can seek God's help to change our responses in those particular situations. Between what happens to us and how we respond or react, there is a moment of choice. When angry feelings emerge we can ask God to help us to control them and to think before we react. Some people like to count to ten . . . really slowly. This can help you to think about what you are going to do before you do it.

REALISTIC EXPECTATIONS

The second action we can take is to embrace realistic expectations about life and people. This is very important. The reality of life is that irritations, frustrations, and hurts are going to happen. Life is not always easy. Stuff happens and we might as well prepare for the irritations that will inevitably come our way. If you think that no one will ever annoy you and that everything will always go perfectly, then those unrealistic expectations will set you up for disappointment and frustration.

The reality is that not everyone will like you. That is annoying because I'm sure you are a really nice person. The reality is that you will be criticised. If you do nothing, you will be criticised. If you do something, you will be criticised. The reality is that life will not always turn out the way you would like it to. There will be obstacles on the way to pursuing your goals, even if they are God-given goals.

I am not saying that we should buy into Murphy's Law. Have you heard of Murphy's Law? Here are a few of Murphy's Laws:

- Nothing is as easy as it looks.
- Everything takes longer than you think.
- Anything that can go wrong, will go wrong.
- If everything seems to be going well, you've obviously overlooked something.
- Every solution breeds new problems.
- The chance of the buttered side of the bread falling face down is directly proportional to the cost of the carpet
- You will always find something in the last place you look.
- No matter how long or how hard you shop for an item, after you have bought it, it will be on sale somewhere else cheaper.
- The other line always moves faster.
- When a broken appliance is demonstrated for the repairman, it will work perfectly.
- Your best golf shots always occur when playing alone. Your worst golf shots always occur when playing with someone you are trying to impress.
- If you are working under your car and drop something, it will always roll to the middle of the car, just out of the reach.
- The intensity of the child's tantrum is directly proportionate to the amount of people around to witness it.

Some people even say that Murphy was an optimist. What's the point? I'm not saying that we should become pessimists. No, we should be realists with an optimistic outlook on life. Bad things do happen in life and if we do not think that they should, we set ourselves up to always be erupting with angry emotions.

In contrast, if we would relax a little more, realising that these sorts of things happen from time to time, we will tend to be less likely to come under the negative influence of anger in our life. The apostle Paul said:

Always be humble and gentle. Be patient with each other, making allowance for each other's faults because of your love (Ephesians 4:2).

He also said:

Make allowance for each other's faults, and forgive anyone who offends you. Remember, the Lord forgave you, so you must forgive others (Colossians 3:13-14).

Some things in life we should just put up with. They are really not that big of a deal. Try to choose not to be offended. Remember, anger is always a choice. There are a whole lot of situations where it really is not worth getting upset. They are beyond our control. They lead to a waste of our energy and a misuse of our anger.

A good question to ask yourself when you are about to become irritated is whether the incident is worth losing your joy over. Jesus came to give us life and joy to the full (John 10:10; 15:11). God's joy is not the same as happiness. Happiness is based on what happens to you. If it happens to be a good day, you are happy. Joy is not based on circumstances.

It is based on our relationship with God and a belief that he is working everything together for our good.

When negative things happen around you, realise that the enemy is trying to pickpocket your joy because the joy of the Lord is your strength (Nehemiah 8:10). Often small things happen and we become upset then suddenly our joy is gone. It is impossible to be angry and joyful at the same time. When we are angry, joy goes out the window.

CHOOSE TO BE A FORGIVING PERSON

Another way to break free from anger is choose to be a forgiving person. Jesus told his followers that it was inevitable that offences would come their way (Matthew 18:7). We are human and we offend one another. There will be conflicts and disagreements. Jesus tells us to prepare for them.

When people hurt us it is not wrong to be upset or to feel pain. Our response is what is most important. We can respond in anger, bitterness and resentment. This is our natural reaction. Someone hurt us, so they owe us and we will make them pay. Unfortunately, this type of response stops the healing process and dramatically affects us - physically, emotionally and spiritually as well as relationally. God never intended for us to live with this kind of destructive poison on the inside.

The other option when we are offended is to choose to forgive. Forgiveness is God's antidote to all hurt. It enables us to release the person and in releasing them we release ourselves. The apostle Paul puts it this way:

Don't sin by letting anger control you. Don't let the sun go
down while you are still angry, for anger gives a foothold to
the devil. Get rid of all bitterness, rage, anger, harsh words
and slander as well as all types of evil behavior. Instead, be
kind to each other, tender-hearted, forgiving one another,
just as God through Christ has forgiven you (Ephesians
4:26-27, 31-32).

Paul tells us to not let the sun go down while we are still
angry. He is giving us twenty-four hours to work on the issue.
That does not mean that we are going to resolve every feeling
of anger within a day. However, we should make sure that
there is a sense of urgency when there has been an offence. We
need to deal with our anger as quickly as possible. We must
not store up our grievances. We need to seek to let forgiveness
flow into the situation.

Forgiveness is important because it helps to preserve
relationships when there has been a time of tension and
conflict. Many relationships are damaged and destroyed
simply because people are more focused on being right than
on restoring the relationship. We need to forgive for the
sake of our relationships and we need to forgive for our own
freedom. When we do not forgive someone, we imprison
ourselves. We tie up our own spirit and we give the devil
a foothold or an access point in our life. When we choose
not to forgive someone, that lack of forgiveness damages us
dramatically, even though the other person may be totally
wrong.

We should also forgive because God has forgiven us. When
teaching his disciples how to pray Jesus made it clear that if

they did not forgive those who offended and hurt them, God would not forgive them (Matthew 6:9-15). This is very challenging. Think about it. If we do not forgive those who offend us, then God will not forgive our sins. There are a lot of Christians today who do not realise the impact of what is happening in their spiritual world when they choose not to forgive those who have offended them.

Forgiveness is not a feeling. It is not something you do because you feel like doing it. It is an act of the will. Because God has forgiven us, we choose to forgive those who have offended us.

Of course, it is easier to forgive someone when they come and apologise to us. However, God never says that we should forgive people only if or when they say that they are sorry. Jesus says that we are to forgive people before they apologise. In fact, the person who has offended us may never apologise for what they have done. We can still choose to forgive. Jesus modelled this on the cross as he forgave his executors (Luke 23:34). Vengeance is God's. Each person will reap the consequences of their own actions. Forgiveness is our responsibility.

Reconciliation is a different thing all together. Unless the person who has offended us apologises, reconciliation may not take place, even though we can adopt a forgiving stance towards them. Some relationships may be unsafe and may require us to set appropriate boundaries for our own protection. However, we can still seek to make every effort to reach out to those who have hurt us, seeking to forgive and to release them, rather than to hold on to a grudge or allow ourselves to become bitter. Asking God to help us forgive those who have offended us and to release grace into our lives is a powerful way to drain anger from our hearts.

TALK OPENLY AND HONESTLY

Once the emotion of anger has settled down it is important to talk about your feelings with other people. Try to learn from the situation and take steps to avoid it happening again. Speak the truth in a loving manner with the aim of strengthening your relationships. Don't allow emotional distance to remain. Make every effort to reconnect your hearts.

Resolution is best achieved through talking it out. Don't convert angry feelings into angry behavior. Choose an option that helps resolution. Be clear about the source of your anger and direct the solution to this source. Confrontation always works better after forgiveness, not before it.

Avoid pushing down your feelings of anger (repression). The problem with this is that if you bury the anger deep enough, it will eventually break out in various ways. This is dangerous because there has been no resolution to the anger.

Don't give uncontrolled expression to your anger through your behavior (ventilation). Some people believe that this helps to drain the reservoir of accumulated anger. Secular marriage counselors have even been known to give husbands and wives rubber baseball bats to fight with. Of course, this has been discovered to be utterly useless because it only helps the person rehearse their anger, which often results in the anger growing (they pick up a real bat). Ventilation often relieves the angry surge but it does not deal with the cause of the anger. Sin is usually in the behavior you choose when you are angry.

It is far better and far healthier to control your feelings of anger and to choose not to vent them through angry behaviour. Once your emotions have cooled, try to talk about the issues in a constructive rather than a destructive manner.

When communicating about our anger it is important to realise it is often not *what* we say that gets us into trouble but *how* we say it. In other words, the content may be right but the delivery can damage any opportunity to restore the relationship. This is a problem in many relationships and it often hinders issues from being resolved adequately.

Sometimes talking with someone else about your anger, such as a counsellor or mature Christian, can also be helpful. If we get stuck, we should ask for help. It's as simple as that.

BE QUICK TO APOLOGISE

When we use our anger inappropriately it is important to quickly apologise. All of us do things that offend other people from time to time, maybe through our words or our actions. We need to take responsibility for this and ask for forgiveness. When we apologise, it helps drain further anger out of a situation. However, when there's pride in our hearts, we refuse to take personal responsibility. We blame the other person for what they've done while justifying ourselves. In contrast, if we walk in humility, we will courageously look at our own mistakes, our own lack of sensitivity and we will do our best to rectify the situation.

Almost fifty percent of marriages today end in divorce. It is interesting to note that having disagreements or arguments is not necessarily hazardous to a marriage. In fact, a good disagreement can contribute to the working through of differences in a marriage. The primary issue is whether a couple can remain emotionally connected after a disagreement. If couples turn away from each other, instead of towards each other, the marriage is in trouble. The number one predictor of divorce is not fighting. It is emotional disconnection, which means that after an argument has finished there is no reconnection of hearts. Once that emotional bond is broken, unless it's repaired, the relationship is at risk.

Gary Smalley teaches people how to untie someone else's internal knots of anger. First, become soft and tender. Proverbs 15:1 says, "A gentle answer deflects anger, but harsh words make tempers flare." The very physiology of speaking with a soft voice assists in draining anger.

Next, be willing to admit that you're wrong. In most situations, there are wrongs on both sides. We so easily look at what the other person has done to us rather than at ourselves. However, when we apologise for our contribution to the situation, it's like unlocking the key on a pair of tight handcuffs. It releases and brings relief into the situation. Sometimes we may not be wrong in what we've done, but maybe the way we went about it didn't help.

As parents our discipline of our children may be right but we may have overreacted and disciplined in anger. The discipline may have been appropriate but the way we went about it created distance between us and that child. If so, we need to repair the situation and this may include apologising.

When you apologise, it is important to choose the right wording. Learn to say, "I was wrong." They are three very powerful words. Another important phrase is, "Would you forgive me?" Don't say, "If I offended you ..." What that is saying is, "I don't think I've done anything wrong but if you think so ..." That doesn't really help much at all.

Don't say, "I was wrong, but you were too." That usually gets the argument going all over again. Making an appropriate and an effective apology is essential to reconnecting emotionally and rebuilding any relationship.

We also need to do our best to understand each situation from the other person's perspective. Try to put yourself in their shoes. Ask yourself what you would be thinking and feeling if you were them. This can be a great aid to conflict resolution.

Not long after I became senior minister of a church in Melbourne, Australia back in 1995, we were having a prayer time for people after a Sunday church meeting. We had trained a group of people as our prayer team and I called them forward to pray for people in need. A man in the church who was a bit of a maverick came forward to pray for people even though he wasn't part of our prayer ministry team. We were all worshipping God and praying for people. I looked over and saw him praying for someone and I was really annoyed. I immediately went over to him and confronted him about how he shouldn't be doing that because he wasn't on the prayer team. It was fairly heated but he eventually went back to his seat and we went on ministering to people. He was really upset and so was I.

After the church meeting I went home and had lunch with my family. As I was telling my wife Nicole about what had happened, I felt prodded by the Holy Spirit. As I reflected honestly, I realised that I was right in what I did, in that he shouldn't have been praying for people at this time. However, I didn't go about it the best way, in that I confronted him in public and in somewhat of a reactionary manner. I immediately went to the phone and called this man. I told him that I was sorry for how I spoke to him and for doing so in public. I then asked him to forgive me. It went quiet for a few seconds and then we were able to resolve the issue, with him also apologising for pushing himself forward. You could feel the anger and the tension drain out of the situation. It was the right thing for me to do and it felt good too.

This may seem like a small thing but learning to apologise when necessary has great power to maintain and strengthen all relationships. Even if you think that you are ten percent wrong and the other person is ninety percent wrong, take care of your part. You go first. Yes, it takes humility but if we value our relationships, learning to be quick to apologise is vital.

FREEDOM FROM ANGER

We all get angry from time to time. How do you handle your feelings of anger? What's it like? Is it constructive or is it destructive? Do you have any strained relationships right now? If so, what could you do to bring about some more warmth and love into those relationships?

Who do you need to forgive right now? Is your inner emotional world tied up in knots? If someone has offended you and you haven't forgiven them, you can receive prayer and you can go for counselling, but until you obey God's word and forgive that person you won't know the freedom and the release that you're longing for. Remember that Jesus said:

God blesses those who work for peace, for they will be called the children of God (Matthew 5:9).

PRAYER

Let me pray for you.

"Father, I pray that you would free us from every prison of anger today. Show us any anger triggers that we may have. Free us from unrealistic expectations about life and people. Help us to forgive those who have hurt or offended us. We release them to you. We want to be quick to apologise when we have been wrong. Teach us to repair and rebuild any relationships. May we be peacemakers, just like you, in Jesus name. Amen."

REFLECTION QUESTIONS

1. Discuss your family background and upbringing. Was anger a common emotion in your home? How was it expressed? How was it handled?

2. How do you personally deal with angry feelings? Do you tend to let them out quickly or do you tend to bury them inside?

3. Reflect on a time when you got really angry. What happened and how did it all end up?

4. Imagine you've recently had a big argument with someone. What are some actions you could take to build a bridge and reconnect with that person emotionally?

5. Why is forgiveness so difficult?

6. What are some situations that we should be "righteously angry" about?

CHAPTER FOUR

FREEDOM FROM FEAR

⬆

A few years ago our family was holidaying on a beautiful island in Fiji. Most days were spent eating, sleeping, reading, swimming and snorkeling. It was one of our best times together as a family.

One day I was snorkeling with our son Ashley and our daughter Natasha. There was a pontoon about twenty metres from the shore which was a good place to snorkel because there were always lots of fish there. Further out there were reefs and coral and more exotic fish to find.

We decided to head out from the pontoon to see what other fish we could see. We swam approximately one hundred metres out from the pontoon, then stopped and chatted together for a minute. Then we all dived down. I swam down deep and saw lots of beautiful fish. Eventually, I came back to the surface for air then went down again. After a few dives I came up, took off my goggles and looked around. I saw Ashley but Natasha was nowhere in sight. I did a quick 360 degree spin but couldn't see her anywhere. Ashley came up and I said, "Where's Natasha?" I started to panic. I dove down again, looking in all directions for her. She was nowhere to be found.

I came to the surface again and started yelling, "Natasha, Natasha!" I was so afraid. Had she drowned? Had we lost her? What was I going to do? My heart was pounding furiously. Ashley didn't know where she was either.

We had looked under the water. We had looked on the surface of the water. She was gone. We swam as fast as we could back to the pontoon. As we approached I suddenly saw her, splashing around with some new friends she had made. I was so relieved. As it turned out, as Ashley and I had dived under, she decided to head back to the pontoon. My heart started to return to its normal rate. It was a scary experience. Thankfully, my fears were relieved.

Fear is a common emotion. In fact, it's probably one of the first childhood emotions that we experience. I remember, as a little boy, having a fear of the dark. I needed a light on in the hallway outside my bedroom and my door open so that I could see the light in order for me to have any chance of going to sleep. We lived in an old two storey house for a few years and sometimes when trying to sleep I would think that I could hear footsteps on the stairs. Was it someone coming to get me? No, it was just my own heart beat, which seemed to get louder and louder as my imagination went wild. At other times, I would wonder if someone was under my bed about to grab me. You get the idea.

I am no longer afraid of the dark but a variety of other fears have continued to come my way all of my life. I have had to face the fear of speaking in public, as well as the fear of leading and taking on responsibility. In my early twenties I was up early one morning praying and I had a vision of myself standing in a field. It was night time and I could see dark figures on the edges of this field in all four directions – north, south, east and west. As I continued to pray I sensed that these were four giants trying to keep me from moving out into the inheritance that God had for me. These four words quickly came to my mind: fear, unbelief, discouragement and apathy. I sensed that these were four enemies that I would have to defeat and push back if I was to become all that God intended for me. At the top of the list was fear, a powerful and unrelenting enemy.

THE POWER OF FEAR

The word "fear" comes from the Greek word "phobos". It means dread, terror, to be scared or afraid. Some fears are real while others are imaginary. Natural protective fear can be helpful in keeping us from danger or harm. The fear of the Lord is the beginning of wisdom. The fear of the Lord is being aware that God is watching us at every moment of every day and then living with that awareness. All other fear is destructive and can become like a prison that holds us captive.

There are many different types of fear that people deal with. Fear of heights is common. Many people are more afraid of speaking in public than of spiders. Some people fear confrontation. Others fear small confined spaces. My wonderful mother-in-law used to walk thirty flights of stairs just to avoid getting in a lift or an elevator. Some people fear loud voices because of the association with abuse or scolding. Other people have a fear of failure because they grew up in a home where nothing but perfection was acceptable. Maybe you have a fear of being noticed due to shame in your childhood or hurt and betrayal from authority figures. We can have a fear of intimacy or a fear of close relationship.

One study conducted in America revealed that nearly forty percent of Americans confessed to an extreme fear of an object or situation. The two most common fears were a fear of snakes and a fear of being buried alive. Almost a third of Americans have suffered a panic attack at sometime in their life. One in four said that they had experienced intense fear in social situations such as nervousness, blushing, a racing heart and a dry mouth or throat. These are referred to as social phobias.

Other research indicates that people fear the tax department (57%) more than God (30%); they fear the dentist (58%) more than the doctor (22%); and they fear rats (58%) more than cockroaches (23%). Interestingly, only eleven percent of people who suffer regular intense fears or phobias choose to seek professional help.

THE SOURCE OF FEAR

The first mention of fear in the Bible is in the book of Genesis. God created the world, including humans, and he placed Adam and Eve in the Garden of Eden. It was a peaceful paradise of perfect relationships. Into this environment came Satan in the form of a serpent. Satan is the father of lies and he slanders and twists God's word. He tempted them to disobey God's clear command (Genesis 3:1-7). As a result of their disobedience, they became afraid and they hid themselves from God (Genesis 3:8-10). Fear is one of the primal dysfunctions that entered into humanity's heart because of sin. In fact, almost all sins such as lying, greed, slander, gossip and pride, emerge out of a root of fear. Fear continues to plague us to this day.

THE EFFECTS OF FEAR

The effects of fear throughout human history are devastating. Fear has led to war, murder, violence and rage. Every conflict reflects some sort of fear. International politics is often a story of intimidation and fear. Today, we face an even darker enemy in the form of terrorism. Fear grips many people's hearts. You can almost smell it and you can see it on people's faces in many countries of the world. Many people are on edge because fear is tying them in knots.

Fear causes people to behave irrationally. Fear can lead to people misrepresenting God. Fear can cause great damage to relationships. At a personal level, fear can also paralyse us. It can immobilise, terrorise and keep us from stepping out into new things.

In J.R.R. Tolkien's epic story, *The Lord of the Rings*, there is a scene where the hobbit Frodo Baggins enters the lair of a huge spider named Shelob. She bites him and immediately Frodo is paralysed. The spider then spins a web around him. Although he's alive, he looks like a dead person.

When his good friend, Samwise Gamgee, comes along, he is convinced that Frodo is dead. This is what fear does to us. It stings us. It paralyses us. We feel like we can hardly breathe.

There is another Iranian tale about the Mongolian invasion back in the Twelfth Century. A Mongolian was walking through one of the cities in Iran and he came upon a crowd of hapless locals. He wanted to kill them but he didn't bring his sword. So he told those ten people to wait there while he went and got his sword to kill them. They stood there, paralysed in fear.

When Jesus rose from the dead there was a great earthquake. An angel of the Lord came down from heaven, rolled away the stone and sat on it. His face shone like lightning and his clothing was as white as snow. Matthew tells us that the guards "shook with fear when they saw him, and they fell into a dead faint (Matthew 18:1-4)." That's a good description of how fear affects us. Fear paralyses.

The book of Proverbs says:

Fearing people is a dangerous trap, but trusting the Lord means safety (Proverbs 29:25).

The apostle Paul said:

So you have not received a spirit that makes you fearful slaves. Instead, you received God's Spirit when he adopted you as his own children. Now we call him, "Abba, Father (Romans 8:15)."

God clearly desires us as his followers to live lives free from the power of fear.

FEAR NOT!

Many of the people in biblical times who we hold up as heroes of the faith battled with fear. Moses was afraid to go back to Egypt after fleeing in fear forty years earlier (Exodus 3:1 – 4:17). Many of the Israelites were afraid of the giants that were seen in Canaan (Numbers 13:27-33). Gideon was so afraid of his enemies that he went into hiding (Judges 6:11). The disciples were so afraid of the storm attacking their boat that they thought they were going to die (Matthew 8:4-26).

No wonder God so frequently had to say to people, "Fear not!" There are approximately 365 times in the Bible where this statement is said – one for every day of the year. Obviously, this also means that there is something to be afraid of. It's like saying to someone, "Watch out!" This means that there is something to be careful about.

Moving forward in God always involves facing and conquering fear. At every new level there is usually a new devil waiting to intimidate us and keep us from moving on. Remember, there were no giants in the wilderness but as soon as the people of God began to move into their Promised Land, there were giants to face and to defeat. It is the same with us. Complacency involves no fear but advancement always provokes the enemy and requires us to rise above our fears.

CONQUERING FEAR WITH FAITH

David gives us a terrific example of someone who overcame fear through his strong faith in God. His confrontation with Goliath shows us his courage and faith in the face of adversity and fear (1 Samuel 17). Israel and the Philistines were at war, each on a hill with a valley between them. Goliath from Gath was the Philistine champion. He was over nine feet tall with bronze armour and a bronze spear. He had a shield bearer who went ahead of him. Goliath defiantly challenged Israel to come and fight with him. Saul and the Israelites were terrified. For forty days, Goliath came forward every morning and evening and took his stand. He was passionate, intense and unrelenting in his attack. He was determined to intimidate and destroy God's people.

This was a challenge that in the natural seemed impossible. Saul, the leader of the nation, was afraid and did not know what to do. As a result, the people were afraid and discouraged. They cowered before Goliath in great fear. David now enters the scene.

David was the youngest of eight sons born to Jesse and he had the responsibility of tending his father's sheep at Bethlehem. His three older brothers were in Saul's army. Jesse sent David to see how the battle was progressing. There are four lessons we can learn from how David rose up in faith to conquer the spirit of fear that was imprisoning so many people.

FACE YOUR FEARS

First, David had a warrior spirit of faith that motivated him to face the fear. His first words were:

Who is this pagan Philistine anyway, that he is allowed to defy the armies of the living God (1 Samuel 17:26)? When he spoke with Saul, his first words were:

Don't worry about this Philistine. I'll go fight him (1 Samuel 17:32)!

David refused to be intimidated by what he saw with his eyes or the natural circumstances. He looked at this challenge with the eyes of faith and with a confidence in God's ability to do the impossible.

Intimidation came at David from every direction - from his older brother Eliab who seemed jealous and envious of David, from King Saul who looked down on him because of his youthfulness and from Goliath himself who ridiculed him. Yet, inspite of all of this attack, David refused to run away or hide. He faced his fear head on. He refused to retreat. In fact, he ran toward Goliath with a spirit of faith.

We must not run from our fears or try to hide from them. To conquer our fears we need to admit that we have them. Unless we face our fears head on, we will never overcome them.

TRUST IN GOD

Second, David had great confidence and trust in God. He saw victory as a certainty and his personal faith in God was enough to carry the nation forward into victory. He was strong in the midst of the intimidation, doubt and unbelief of everyone who was around him. David's faith was not in his own ability. His act of defiance was not a sign of a big ego or even of extreme self-confidence. His faith and trust was in the living God. Notice his words:

> David replied to the Philistine, "You come to me with sword, spear and javelin, but I come to you in the name of the Lord of Heaven's Armies—the God of the armies of Israel, whom you have defied. Today the Lord will conquer you, and I will kill you and cut off your head. And then I will give the dead bodies of your men to the birds and wild animals, and the whole world will know that there is a God in Israel! And everyone assembled here will know that the Lord rescues his people, but not with sword and spear. This is the Lord's battle, and he will give you to us (1 Samuel 17:45-47)!"

We can have the same trust in God as we face our personal fears. God has promised to be with us all the time, no matter what happens (Matthew 28:20). Even in the midst of a storm, he is there with us. Our life is not subject to fate or chance. We are in the hands of a sovereign God. We can trust in him and his providential care. God is in control.

As followers of Christ, Jesus is the initiator and finisher of our faith (Hebrews 12:1-2). He is the one on whom our faith depends from start to finish. Our faith is not in ourselves or in other people. The more we see Jesus as he really is, the more our faith in him will increase. Like Peter walking on the water, we need to keep our eyes fixed on Jesus. We can trust fully in him.

REMEMBER THE WORKS OF GOD

Third, notice that David strengthened his faith by reflecting on previous times that God had helped him face fear and intimidation. He recalled to mind the times when God had delivered him from the attack of a bear and a lion (1 Samuel 17:34, 37). These smaller victories gave him assurance that God would do the same with this new larger challenge in front of him.

We also need to recall to our minds God's mighty deeds. It is easy to forget what he has done on our behalf when we face new challenges. In Old Testament times, the nation of Israel often established altars as places of remembrance of God's mighty works. These served as reminders for themselves and the generations to come. They were established to create faith for future challenges.

When our oldest son, Josiah, was a small boy, I remember asking him to jump from halfway up the stairs and I would catch him – just for fun. He didn't want to jump because he thought I'd drop him. After assuring him multiple times that I wouldn't drop him, he hesitatingly jumped. I caught him and he ran up the stairs to do it again. This time he was a little less afraid, so he jumped again. We did this a number of times and his confidence grew each time. In fact, he used to try to jump even when I wasn't there! In the same way, our confidence in Father God grows as we experience him catching us through multiple life experiences.

BELIEVE THE PROMISES OF GOD

Finally, David knew and believed the covenant promises of the God of Israel. He knew that the God that Israel worshipped was the Lord of all the earth and that he would vindicate his people who place their trust in him. There was no doubt in his mind. He also knew that he had been anointed by the prophet Samuel to advance God's purposes in his generation. He saw it as the Lord's battle and he stepped out in full confidence (1 Samuel 17:45-47).

We also have great and precious promises from God as we face our fears. God's Word is his will revealed. It contains his promises for our lives. Today there are many voices and many words being spoken at us. Many of them erode our faith in God. Thankfully, we can tune into God's Word. Hearing God's word creates faith inside of us (Romans 10:17). As we hear and believe his word our faith grows. That's why it's so important to meditate and think about God's promises.

Don't let Satan put fear in your heart and stop you from doing what God wants you to. Believe that you are who God says you are and you can do what he says you can do. God is with you and he will keep his promises to you. Here are some encouraging promises about victory over fear:

I prayed to the Lord, and he answered me. He freed me from all my fears (Psalm 34:4).

The wicked run away when no one is chasing them, but the godly are as bold as lions (Proverbs 28:1).

When I am afraid, I will put my trust in you. I praise God for what he has promised. I trust in God, so why should I be afraid? What can mere mortals do to me (Psalm 56:3-4)?

We can renew and reprogram our thinking with the words of God. This requires us to challenge the thoughts that come into our mind, many of which have become patterns developed since childhood. As we do we create faith that can help us rise up above every fear. The battle for freedom takes place in our mind. We have nothing to fear but fear itself.

Imagine waking up one morning and going to your backyard and for some reason a stray pit bull has made its home there. It snarls and growls at you. You're terrified. You have a choice to make. You can live your whole life never entering your backyard because there is a stray pit bull there. Or you can have a pit bull D-day. This pit bull is not your pit bull. You can take a stand. Wouldn't you rather be in heaven with scars from a fight with the pit bull, having eliminated him, than to live your whole life terrified and never entered your backyard which was yours to enjoy?

In the same way, we need to start challenging each thought that comes our way, especially thoughts of fear. Refuse to allow them to overwhelm your life. In Christ, you are more than a conqueror. God has given you weapons to fight the good fight of faith (2 Corinthians 10:3-5). No longer listen to the lies of the enemy that tell you that you'll never break free from fear.

God has placed everything in heaven and earth under the authority of Jesus Christ (Colossians 2:10). When we take our place in Christ, we too can have authority over every fear that seeks to hinder us. We can rise up and challenge our thinking. We don't have to allow thoughts of fear and intimidation to bully us. We can stand up against them and confront them in the name of Jesus.

David's story shows us how the faith of one person led to victory and then the entire nation's confidence rose. One person stepped forward and God brought a great victory. David won the battle because he faced his fear, he trusted in God, he believed God's promises, and he remembered the works of God. He conquered fear and led an entire nation into victory (1 Samuel 17:48-54).

FACING OUR CHALLENGES

As we seek to move forward into all that God has for us, we too have an enemy who seeks to intimidate us in the same way that Goliath came against the Israelites. The apostle Peter tells us that the devil is like a roaring lion prowling around seeking to devour us (1 Peter 5:8). We need to be watchful and resist him. The apostle Paul tells us that we should be familiar with Satan's evil schemes so that he does not outsmart us (2 Corinthians 2:11). Satan frequently puts giants in our way to intimidate and hinder us.

Our giants are not physical giants, as our battle is not against flesh and blood. They are spiritual forces arrayed against us. Our weapons are not physical but spiritual (Ephesians 6:12; 2 Corinthians 10:3-6). Giants can represent the challenges we face in our lives. They may be situations, circumstances, or even people who come against us to intimidate us and hold us back.

Giants are bigger and stronger than us. We must not underestimate their ability to destroy us. We must drive them away and break out into new territory. Each giant can be conquered and subdued only through the power of the Holy Spirit and the Word of God. The Spirit comes to give us the necessary weapons and power to overcome.

What is interesting is that the very process of facing and dealing with life's challenges is how we become strong people. We can't develop strength without pressure and without a degree of stress. The hard times have the potential to make us strong.

Make every effort not to give in or come apart under a particular challenge. Give your best efforts to face it head on and believe for a solution. Give it your best prayers, your best thinking and your best energy. There is always something we can do to either completely conquer the challenge or at least minimise its impact. Sometimes there are tough choices to be made, changes to be embraced and maybe even compromises where we have to choose less than the ideal. Sometimes we need to try a different approach – a different tack. Look at the challenge in an alternative way or do something different about it. We must not ignore our challenges or allow ourselves to be overwhelmed by them. We need to refuse to just give up and become a victim. We can determine to be a victor no matter how long it takes.

We can draw on God's strength. God always makes his grace available for us when facing challenges. In fact, he always sends more than enough grace for what we are going through. Sometimes in the moment we may not feel it, but when looking back, we'll see it – amazing sustaining grace. Grace – it's not just about salvation; it's about life. Grace is God's goodness but it is also his ability and his strength to cope (2 Corinthians 12:7-10).

We can choose to be optimistic about the future. We can expect everything to work out well and in the meantime embrace a high tolerance for ambiguity and uncertainty (Jeremiah 29:11, 2 Corinthians 4:15-18). Otherwise, if we are not careful, challenges have a way of subtly draining away our sense of hope. It's like the pressures or realities of today blind us from seeing any relief tomorrow. We can slowly begin to believe that nothing will change or that the challenges may never go away. Let's be very clear – just choosing to be optimistic doesn't guarantee that the challenges will go away but we can believe that even if they don't, God's grace will carry us through.

As we take these steps, our faith will grow. Yes, faith is measurable (2 Thessalonians 1:3, 2 Corinthians 10:15). The Bible speaks of "no faith", "little faith", "weak faith", "dead faith", "great faith", "full of faith" and "strong faith". Like the disciples of Jesus, let's pray, "Lord, increase our faith" (Luke 17:5). As our faith grows, our victory over fear will be more decisive.

BREAKING THE SPIRIT OF FEAR

One of my favourite Bible verses is in a letter that the apostle Paul wrote to a young team member named Timothy. Timothy's personality was shy by nature and he lacked a great deal of confidence. Paul said to him:

> For God did not give us a spirit of fear and timidity, but of power, love, and self-discipline (2 Timothy 1:7).

Timothy was a young leader who was serving as an apostolic representative in a well-established church in the city of Ephesus. He was given a specific task by Paul to set the church in order. This involved providing leadership to some older people and leaders. Paul writes to encourage him to not allow himself to be intimidated but to remember the resources available to him through the indwelling Holy Spirit, the Helper (John 14:17, 26; 15:26; 16:13-15).

The Holy Spirit comes to break the power of fear in our life. The word "timidity" means fear, reticence or cowardice (a lack of courage). Fear will limit us and hinder us from fulfilling our God-given destiny. Fear, timidity, insecurity and inferiority have to be broken. God wants to put a confidence, an assurance and a faith inside of us.

We need to step out and face our fears. Courage is not the absence of fear but the conquering of it. Instead of fear, the Spirit of God who lives inside of us comes to give us all the resources we need, including power, love and wisdom. As our Helper, we need to call on the Spirit's assistance, rather than seeking to face our fears alone. He always comes when we call.

PERFECT LOVE

One of the greatest weapons that God gives us to overcome fear is a revelation of the love of God. It may sound overly simple but the realisation that we are in the hands of an Almighty God who loves us can set us free from all fear. God's love is revealed through the person of Jesus Christ. Jesus shows us what God is like. When you look at Jesus you see someone who loves people and seeks to help them become free from everything that binds them or holds them down. He reaches out to the hurting, the broken and the wounded with great compassion, mercy and kindness.

The greatest display of Christ's love for us was when he willingly took our place on that cross. He took our punishment upon himself. Surprisingly, God did this while we were still sinners and before we had any interest in him (Romans 5:8). When we have a revelation of God's incredible love for us it can change our focus. The apostle John, one of Jesus' closest disciples puts it this way:

> We know how much God loves us and we have put our trust in his love. God is love and all who live in love live in God and God lives in them. And as we live in God, our love grows more perfect. So we will not be afraid on the day of judgment, but we can face him with confidence because we live like Jesus here in this world. Such love has no fear, because perfect love expels all fear. If we are afraid, it is for fear of punishment and this shows that we have not fully experienced his perfect love. We love each other because he loved us first (1 John 4:16-19).

Perfect love dispels all fear. That is powerful. When we fully recognise and embrace God's amazing love for us, it has the power to free us from every prison of fear. Love provides a sense of safety, security and confidence because we are in God's hands.

In Christ, we have a new freedom. It is a freedom from fear, a freedom from condemnation and a freedom from dread. Jesus is the personification of God's love towards us. John tells us that:

> God loved the world so much that he gave his one and only Son, so that everyone who believes in him will not perish but have eternal life (John 3:16).

Come to him. Accept him as your Saviour - the forgiver of your sin. This is the beginning of freedom from all fear.

PRAYER

Let's pray about fear.

"Father, I pray right now for anyone who is reading this book who is battling with fear. I pray that they would take hold of the truth of your word. Every spirit of fear must go in the name of Jesus. We receive your love. We take hold of our freedom.

Your word is true no matter what circumstance we may be in or no matter what we are going through. You are with us. You gave your only Son for us. Through him we can conquer fear. May your love overwhelm us and drive out all fear. All fear must bow before Jesus. Everything must come under his authority. Amen."

REFLECTION QUESTIONS

1. What fears have you overcome so far in your life? What were some contributing factors to your victory?

2. What are the biggest fears you are battling with right now? What lessons can you apply from your past to your current situation?

3. What are some promises from God's Word that you can read and meditate on regularly to help you overcome your fears? Try Psalm 91 and Romans 8:31-39 as starters. Write or type out your own list of promises and commit them to memory.

4. What are some ways that you can turn fear around to become a positive thing in your life? For example, fear can make you more dependent on God and fear can be a catalyst to grow faith in your life if you face it head on.

5. Who could be a help to you in overcoming your fears?

6. What small steps could you take to face your fears head on?

7. If you had no fear, what would you do with your life? Why not face that fear with a spirit of faith in God and go for it!

CHAPTER FIVE

FREEDOM FROM DEPRESSION

↑

Back in 2002, I went through what could be called an emotional valley. It took everything within me to get through the day. Each appointment, meeting, task or project seemed like an insurmountable mountain that I had to somehow climb. I was relieved when something was over and I did not experience much joy or pleasure during any of these activities. It was like a cloud had settled in over my heart and mind. Everything was bleak, like someone had closed the window shutters.

In the natural, nothing was going wrong. My family life was good, as was church, work and ministry. I was not backslidden and I could not think of anything that I had done wrong. There had been no tragedies or disasters in my life either. As a result, I was not sure whether this was the devil or God, whether it was a spiritual wilderness or some sort of a mid-life crisis. I was confused.

After a time of reflection and with some help from other people I came to realise that I had been suffering from a form of depression, most likely a type of adrenaline exhaustion, due to living my life at a pace that was not sustainable. My emotions were basically shutting down and refusing to continue to live at such a pace. I had to make some adjustments.

I was not able to snap out of this season. A quick prayer did not fix it. It took some time and some adjustments, along with help and support from other people, till eventually I came up out of that valley. The clouds cleared and the shades came up. Life returned to normal again.

I have not been back in that valley since then, but there have been a couple of times where I have been very near the edge. I can read my emotions a lot better now. As a result, I have been able to make adjustments so that I do not go back there again.

What about you? Have you ever been depressed? Maybe you have but you did not recognise it as depression. We have all experienced times of at least mild depression at some time in our life and more likely than not, quite frequently. Your favourite sports team loses, you fail a test, a friend moves away or you have a difficult day. However, this type of mild depression usually passes within a few days or even hours. However, sometimes depression can settle in for weeks, months and even years in certain situations.

SYMPTOMS OF DEPRESSION

Depression is a complex subject, as it can take on many different forms and it has a variety of causes, as well as symptoms. Unlike a physical injury or illness, depression is hard to 'see', but it is no less painful or difficult to work through. Depression affects people in a wide variety of different ways. Symptoms of depression may include a negative change in thought, in mood or in behaviour. Depression can happen to everyone in varying degrees or levels - from mild (feeling 'down') to very serious (being suicidal).

When it comes to a person's thinking, depression causes people to be far more negative and pessimistic. Small obstacles can become almost insurmountable. It can be difficult to concentrate.

Mood changes include feeling sadder. A depressed person becomes discouraged and at times overwhelmed. They lose the ability to enjoy activities that they normally would. In fact, the ability to experience pleasure is dramatically affected by depression.

Behaviour changes include becoming quite lethargic. There is a high degree of fatigue. A depressed person often feels sleepy and lacks energy to make decisions. These are some of the common symptoms of a person experiencing a bout of depression.

CAUSES OF DEPRESSION

Where does depression come from? There are many possible causes of depression. Sometimes depression comes from stress. Life can be tough. Life can be difficult.

I was driving my car recently, on the way to pick up my son from his work. I came to an intersection and bang, there was this huge accident right in front of me. Thankfully, no-one was seriously hurt. I am sure that for those people involved in that accident, it was a stressful day. They would have experienced some low mood for a while, especially the young girl who was responsible for the accident. Her car was in a mess and she was really shaken up. Sometimes just the stress of life and the various crises that come along can be a cause of depressing emotions.

Sometimes it can be grief that causes depression. If you have ever lost a loved one, you will know what it is to go through a period of low mood and to feel down because of the loss. Or maybe it is losing something else that is valuable in our life.

Anger can cause depression, as can disappointment, guilt, fear and negativity. Sometimes it is adrenaline exhaustion, which was what happened in my case. I was living at a crazy pace and trying to do too much. There can also be genetic causes of depression or biological issues such as brain chemistry. Some forms of depression may require anti-depressant medication to help bring about normal chemical balance in a person's physical body. So we can see that there is a wide variety of causes of depression.

Depression is an age-old problem, although in our generation there is an unprecedented epidemic of depression.

It is a universal problem and it is no respecter or persons. It is everywhere. Depression is often referred to as 'the common cold of the emotions', because it seems to be so frequent that many people are catching it. It is very possible that either you or someone you know may have to battle with some form of depression at some time.

It is estimated that one in eight men will have a severe bout of depression somewhere in their life and one in three women will have a severe bout of depression. Women are twice as likely to get depressed as men. There are a lot of theories about why this is the case. Someone sent me an email recently with a humorous explanation as to why men are never depressed. Here it is, just for a bit of fun.

Why men are never depressed:
- The same hairstyle lasts for years, maybe decades;
- Phone conversations are over in 30 seconds flat;
- Car mechanics tell you the truth;
- Same work, more pay;
- Wedding dress $5000, tux rental $100;
- One mood all the time;
- A five day holiday requires only one suitcase;
- You can open all of your own jars;
- You get extra credit for the slightest act of thoughtfulness;
- If someone forgets to invite you, he or she can still be your friend;
- Your underwear is $8.95 for a three pack;

- You only have to shave your face and neck;
- You don't have to stop and think which way to turn a nut on a bolt;
- You can do your nails with a pocket-knife;
- You can do your Christmas shopping for 25 relatives on December 24 in 25 minutes;

No wonder men never get depressed!

Well, that is one theory! Humour aside, one of the reasons women become more depressed than men is that women tend to feel their depression. Men tend to act out their depression more than they feel it. Sometimes when men are depressed, they may not feel sad, but they may become irritable or angry. They may also immerse themselves in their work or become involved in adrenaline producing activities that may become addictive. Because men do not feel their depression as much as women, they often do not recognise it. However, both men and women are affected by depression or by low moods.

ATTITUDES ABOUT DEPRESSION

Unfortunately, there is a stigma attached to depression, along with a great deal of ignorance and misunderstanding. Some people think that depression is a sign of weakness and that strong people never get depressed. This is simply not true.

Winston Churchill was one of the great political and military leaders of the twentieth century. He led the allied forces in World War II to victory over Hitler. Yet he suffered regularly with depression. In fact, he labelled his depression, "the black dog." There were many days in his life when the black dog was in the room. There were other days when it was gone. Churchill was not a weak person yet he suffered from depression.

Martin Luther, the influential leader of the Protestant Reformation, had regular battles with depression. Charles Spurgeon, one of the greatest preachers of all time, also had regular battles with depression. In his book, *Lectures to My Students*, he has a whole chapter called "The Minister's Fainting Fits," where he talks about battling with various emotions such as depression. Depression is not a sign of weakness.

Some people think that depression is a result of sin (God's punishment or withdrawal from you) or that depression in itself is a sin. People who believe this would say that a depressed person needs to repent, snap out of it and get a good attitude. Yes, there may be times when depression is a consequence of decisions that a person has made, but most often that is not the reason why someone suffers from depression.

Some people think that if you are depressed it means that you have no faith. People make comments such as, "If you had more faith, then you would live on the mountain tops all the time. You would be victorious and you would never feel down." Have you ever thought that? This is not really true. In fact, I talked to a woman recently who said to me, "You know, when you are working through depression, you do not lack faith. It is your faith that keeps you going. What you lack is hope!" What a powerful statement. Depression is rarely a sign of a lack of faith. People suffering from depression are often hanging tightly onto God. What they need is some hope that they will be able to come out of that valley.

Some people think that depression is demonic. It simply needs to be rebuked. Obviously, there may be certain cases where this may be the case, but it is unwise to think that all depression is a "spiritual attack."

No doubt, these negative attitudes towards depression can really damage people's lives if we are not careful. In contrast, Christian psychologist Arch Hart believes that depression can be a healing emotion if we co-operate with it. It is part of our body's warning system, calling attention to something that is wrong. It slows us down so that healing can follow. Depression is the cry of the soul that something is missing.

BIBLICAL EXAMPLES OF DEPRESSION

God has a lot to say about the practical areas of our life, including depression. If you look up at the word 'depression' in the concordance, you will not find many verses in the Bible on depression, but the concept of discouragement, despair, low mood and depression are mentioned frequently throughout. In fact, some of the heroes of the faith experienced depression, including people such as Job who had some pretty down days (Job 6:8-9; 7:16; 10:1).

What about Moses? Moses was a phenomenal leader but there were days when he wanted to die and kill everyone else in his world (Numbers 11:10-15). Have you ever had one of those days? What about Jeremiah? Jeremiah was called to preach but no one responded to his message. One time he said:

Cursed be the day that I was born (Jeremiah 20:7-18)!

Now that is what I call feeling pretty low. David also experienced frequent times of difficulty and depressed emotions (Psalm 40:1-2; 43:5).

Job, Moses, Jeremiah, David - these were not weak people. These were not people without faith. Yet they went through experiences of depression that they had to work through.

A DEPRESSED PROPHET

Let us look a bit more in depth at one person in Bible times that went through an incredible battle with depression. His name is Elijah. Yes, the great prophet Elijah. Elijah was a prophet in Israel during the time of King Ahab. Ahab was backslidden and most of the nation was worshipping a foreign god by the name of Baal. Elijah preached during this time and there had been no rain for three years because of God's judgment on the people's sin.

After this, Elijah called for a confrontation. He told the people that they had to make a decision. They could not continually go back and forth. They had to either serve God or serve Baal. He challenged them to get off the fence.

Elijah called the entire nation up to Mount Carmel. He told four hundred and fifty of the prophets of Baal to come up the mountain too. He took two bulls and challenged them to a sacrifice. The God who answered by fire was who they were going to serve. This would make a great movie!

Elijah told the prophets of Baal to go first. They selected a bull, prepared the sacrifice then started crying out to their god to answer by fire. The whole morning went by and nothing happened. No breath of wind, no fire, nothing. Then they became pretty desperate and started cutting themselves. They were yelling at the top of their voices, crying out to their god Baal.

Then Elijah started teasing them. He taunted them, suggesting that maybe their god was on holidays or still asleep. He told them to yell a little louder. Maybe they needed to wake him up. Eventually it was Elijah's turn. He put the bull on the altar. He asked the servants to pour water over it a few times. Then he began to pray and fire came down from heaven, consuming the sacrifice and the entire altar.

Elijah then asked the people who they wanted to serve, God or Baal. All of the prophets of Baal were executed and then Elijah heard a sound of rain. He told Ahab to get in his chariot and the Bible tells us that the Spirit of God took a hold of Elijah and he ran faster than the chariot. He was moving - chariots of fire! He ran twenty-seven kilometres to the nearest town of Jezreel. What a day! Elijah was a mighty man of faith and power. That is the background for what we are about to read.

When Ahab got home, he told Jezebel everything Elijah had done, including the way he had killed all the prophets of Baal. So Jezebel sent this message to Elijah: "May the gods strike me and even kill me if by this time tomorrow I have not killed you just as you killed them."

Elijah was afraid and fled for his life. He went to Beersheba, a town in Judah, and he left his servant there. Then he went on alone into the wilderness, traveling all day. He sat down under a solitary broom tree and prayed that he might die. "I have had enough, Lord," he said. "Take my life, for I am no better than my ancestors who have already died." Then he lay down and slept under the broom tree (1 Kings 19:1-5).

Elijah was now in Beersheba, which is 145 kilometres south of Jezreel. He was sitting under a broom tree, which was about four metres tall with long branches. He had come down from the mountain top into a deep valley of despair. In fact, he was so depressed that he had become suicidal. He wanted to die. He wanted to end it all.

As we continue this story, we are going to look for some principles as to how God helped Elijah work through his depression. Remember, the Apostle Paul told us that everything written in the Old Testament was written for our benefit (1 Corinthians 10:1-11). Although this is a narrative, there are lessons that we can glean from it.

I realise that there are different types of depression but there are some insights here in Elijah's journey that I believe can help each one of us today. God did not judge Elijah for his depressed feelings but he did send him some appropriate treatment to help him out. Let's use the word HOPE as an acronym and draw four principles out of the story for finding freedom from depression.

HONOUR YOUR BODY

The first step in dealing with depression is to honour your physical body. Let's keep reading.

> Then (Elijah) lay down and slept under the broom tree. But as he was sleeping, an angel touched him and told him, "Get up and eat!" He looked around and there beside his head was some bread baked on hot stones and a jar of water! So he ate and drank and lay down again. Then the angel of the Lord came again and touched him and said, "Get up and eat some more, or the journey ahead will be too much for you." So he got up and ate and drank, and the food gave him enough strength to travel forty days and forty nights to Mount Sinai, the mountain of God. There he came to a cave, where he spent the night (1 Kings 19:5-9).

Remember, there is nothing in the Bible by accident. Elijah had recently had a mountain top experience but was now depressed. In fact, he was so depressed that he wanted to die. God did not show up but he sent an angel. The angel recognised that Elijah was totally exhausted. He was emotionally and physically worn out. He had been through an incredible high and now he was in this deep low. He was in despair. Notice that the angel first began to attend to Elijah's physical well-being.

It is interesting to note that when we are depressed, we tend to neglect our physical body. If we are going to come out of depression, we need to honour our physical body. The word "honour" means to value, to respect and to look after. Our body is the dwelling place, the house, the temple of God.

The angel let Elijah sleep and get some rest. Sometimes when you are depressed, you need to sleep, you need to rest. The average person needs seven to eight hours of sleep a night. Life is meant to have a rhythm where we alternate between being engaged in activity then disengaging for rest and recovery.

One of the contributing factors to my six month emotional valley was that I had not been living a balanced life. I had not been taking a day off regularly. I had not been making sure that I had time to recover from ministry activity. I would be in India for two weeks mission work, then I would come back and speak at a number of church meetings on the weekend, then I would head off somewhere else overseas for more ministry. I was moving at a pace that could not be sustained.

The angel then brought some food to Elijah. Is this the first reference to angel food cake? Okay, stay with me. The angel cooked up some bread and provided some fresh water.

Scientifically it has been proven that what we eat dramatically affects our well-being. Eating healthy food has a big impact on our overall health and energy. Exercise is important too. Of course, Elijah had had too much exercise. He had run twenty-seven kilometres and he was tired and worn out. The problem in our day is that we usually do not have enough exercise. Of course, when you are depressed, you do not feel like doing anything. Yet, research has proven that engaging in a simple activity, such as taking a walk or playing a sport, increases your physical, emotional and mental well-being.

When you are physically fit and well, you are less prone to becoming depressed in the first place. But if you are experiencing a period of low mood, instead of putting on weight, eating unhealthy foods and avoiding exercise, begin to honour your physical body. It is an important part of coming out of that valley of depression.

We mow our lawns, we clean our houses, we scan our computers for viruses, we repair our appliances but we often do not look after our physical bodies as well as we should. When our physical bodies are run down, it affects our emotions as well as our spiritual well being. Taking time for regular sleep and rest, eating healthy food and engaging in regular physical exercise are all good ways to prevent depression and are also beneficial when we are feeling down. God sent an angel to help Elijah look after himself physically – with sleep, rest, water and healthy food.

OBSERVE YOUR THINKING

The next step in overcoming depression is to observe your thinking. Let's keep reading the story.

> There (Elijah) came to a cave, where he spent the night. But the Lord said to him, "What are you doing here, Elijah?" (1 Kings 19:9)

After the angel attended to Elijah's physical well being, God met personally with Elijah. In the course of conversation, God asked Elijah a question – "What are you doing here?" We need to understand that when God asks a question, it is not because he lacks information.

In the garden, when God asked, "Adam, where are you?," it was not because God could not find where Adam had gone. God is a gifted counsellor. He does not immediately direct Adam. Instead, he asked questions because he wanted Adam to acknowledge where he was.

When Jesus was talking to the disciples, he asked them, "Who do people say that I am (Matthew 16:15)?" Had Jesus forgotten his name? Had he lost his identity? No. He wanted to hear who they thought he was.

When God asked Elijah, "What are you doing here?," he wanted Elijah to observe his own thinking patterns. After Elijah had an encounter with God that included thunder, earthquake, fire and a small still voice, God asked him the same question again. "What are you doing here, Elijah?" (1 Kings 19:13)

Because Elijah was feeling so depressed, his thinking had become distorted. When you are depressed, your thinking becomes very negative. Have you ever been in one of those halls of mirrors, with all those funny mirrors? You look into one and you are twice as tall as you really are. You move on to the next one and you are half as tall. You look like a pygmy. Then the next one, you are about three times as wide. You quickly move on from that one and then have look into one where you are really thin. You tend to stand there for a while.

What is happening? The mirrors are giving you a distorted view of what you really look like. That is how depression affects our thinking. Things that are small become exaggerated. Things that are quite big become minimised.

Look at Elijah's answer to God's question.

Elijah replied, "I have zealously served the Lord God Almighty. But the people of Israel have broken their covenant with you, torn down your altars and killed every one of your prophets. I am the only one left and now they are trying to kill me, too." (1 Kings 19:10)

In answering God's question, Elijah revealed his thinking. Was his thinking accurate? Well, first of all, he had forgotten his experience on the mountain top. Think about it, God answered by fire and all the people said that they would serve God. Elijah had forgotten the great works of God. As a result he had concluded that his work was unfruitful and that his life was not worth living. He had lost confidence in the triumph of God's kingdom and wanted to withdraw from the battle. When you are depressed, you selectively remove the good things that God is doing in your life.

Not only that, Elijah distorted how bad the situation was. He thought that he was the only one left. A little later on, God said to Elijah:

Yet I will preserve 7,000 others in Israel who have never bowed down to Baal or kissed him! (1 Kings 19:18)

The situation is 7000 times better than Elijah had made it out to be. God came and through conversation with Elijah sought to get him to observe his thinking and then begin to bring it into alignment with reality again.

Our thinking has a powerful affect on our feelings and also our behaviour. No wonder the Bible talks about guarding our heart (Proverbs 4:23), renewing our mind (Romans 12:1-2) and taking captive every thought (2 Corinthians 10:5). When we feel low, our thoughts and memories tend to focus on only the negative. This usually makes us feel even worse.

Depression can be similar to a downward spiral. We think negative. We feel negative. We act negative. In fact, it is a cumulative effect. You think depressing thoughts then you feel depressed. You feel depressed then think more depressing thoughts. Then when you think more depressing thoughts, you feel even more depressed. This downward spiral is very hard to break free from.

We need to observe our thoughts and seek to get rid of the depressive bias. The downward spiral needs to be reversed by working to change the negative thinking patterns. As thinking becomes more positive, the depression usually starts to lift and produces more positive thoughts and feelings. Notice that God did not start with Elijah's feelings, which were the symptoms, but rather with his thinking. He went straight to the root of the problem.

Thankfully, the Bible has given us the promise that the Holy Spirit is there to help us renew our mind. We can come to the word of God. That is why reading God's word is so important because it is an accurate mirror that shows us the way things really are. It is not exaggerated nor does it minimise things. It helps us to realign our thinking – about God, ourselves, other people and life in general.

PROVOKE YOURSELF TO ACTION

To break free from depression we first honour our body and then we observe our thinking. The next step is to provoke ourselves to action. Here is what God said next to Elijah.

> Then the Lord told (Elijah), "Go back the same way you came, and travel to the wilderness of Damascus. When you arrive there, anoint Hazael to be king of Aram. Then anoint Jehu son of Nimshi to be king of Israel and anoint Elisha son of Shaphat from the town of Abel-meholah to replace you as my prophet. Anyone who escapes from Hazael will be killed by Jehu and those who escape Jehu will be killed by Elisha! Yet I will preserve 7,000 others in Israel who have never bowed down to Baal or kissed him!" (1 Kings 19:15-19)

God gave Elijah an assignment. He basically told Elijah that it was time to get out of the cave. God recommissioned Elijah to go and complete some tasks for him. He told him to get up and to get to work. Notice that he only gave him three tasks. Not fifty. Three. He was to anoint two kings and then appoint Elisha as the person he would train to succeed him.

Depression tends to make us sluggish and takes away our energy. However, inactivity can get in the way of the healing process. Part of our freedom journey is to get involved once more in daily activities. Even easy tasks can seem hard to do when you are depressed. Pushing yourself to do some activities that you dread or feel too tired to do can help lift the depression. Set yourself some simple tasks that you are no longer doing. It may not be easy but it is important that you re-engage in the activities that you have given up. The sense of tiredness that goes with depression can increase as you do less and as you withdraw. Becoming involved in some simple tasks can help to energise you.

Discover and pursue your purpose in life. Elijah became depressed when he lost a sense of God's calling for his life. He lost perspective and saw no reason to go on. If Elijah had stayed in that cave he probably would have kept going further downhill in his battle with depression.

During my six month valley, I had to slow down and do less but I did keep engaged with life. Even though I did not feel like engaging in some activities, I kept doing them. Keeping in the race, keeping in the rhythm of life, helped me to come out of that valley. You can do the same. Do some simple tasks and keep serving other people.

I read an article recently in which Doctor Carl Menninger, a leading mental health professional, was being interviewed. He was asked what he would advise someone who was about to have a nervous breakdown. Most people thought he would quickly direct the person so see a psychiatrist or a psychologist. Surprisingly, without hesitation, he said, "Tell them to lock up their house, go across the railroad tracks, find somebody in need, and help that person." Here is a leading health professional telling us that if we are struggling with depressing emotions we should get busy helping somebody else. Why? Because when you help somebody else, you climb out of the mire of self pity and you gain proper perspective on your own problems.

That is what God did with Elijah. He helped him get better physically, he worked on his thinking and then he led him back to making a contribution. The kingdom was still moving forward. God had a couple of kings for Elijah to anoint and he needed to find a good successor. God was getting him back on track with his purpose in life. One of the biggest dangers, when we are going through depression, is that we can tend to pull out of the race of life. We need to provoke ourselves to some action.

ESTABLISH SUPPORTIVE RELATIONSHIPS

The final lesson we learn from the story of Elijah is to establish supportive relationships. You will notice that Elijah had left his servant just prior to this episode of depression and during this entire incident, he was alone. Look at the story again.

> Elijah was afraid and fled for his life. He went to Beersheba, a town in Judah, and he left his servant there. Then he went on alone into the wilderness, travelling all day. He sat down under a solitary broom tree and prayed that he might die. "I have had enough, Lord," he said. "Take my life, for I am no better than my ancestors who have already died." (1 Kings 19:3-4)

Notice those words: "He went on alone into the wilderness." Elijah left his servant, his partner in ministry, and it was when he was alone that he hit rock bottom. Loneliness and isolation often feed depression. Sometimes when you are depressed you may not want to be with people but we all need supportive relationships. Part of God's assignment for Elijah was not only to anoint two kings, but to go and find another servant. He was sent to go and recruit Elisha. God was moving Elijah back into the community. He wanted him to experience life and do ministry with other people, not alone. He needed companionship.

We all need friends and close relationships that provide emotional support to us, especially during tough times. It takes time and effort to build strong healthy friendships. We should do this in advance, not just when we are facing depression or other challenges.

As we said in our opening chapter, part of our journey to freedom is moving from isolation into community. If you are going through depression, you need people around you to encourage you, to support you and to provide perspective and a sounding board.

Yes, the word of God is an accurate mirror but sometimes we need people to hear us talk and say, "You know, hold on, that is not really true." We need people to help adjust our thinking. We need friends. We need small groups. We need a church community. Sometimes we need a counsellor, someone who is gifted in understanding an emotion such as depression and who can sit with us and talk it through so that we get the help we need. Occasionally, we need medical doctors, especially if our depression is severe.

These people are all a part of our support team. Do not isolate yourself from people. You need relationships even more than ever when you are going through times of depression.

HOPE FOR THE FUTURE

The inspiring thing about Elijah is that, despite his incredible bout of depression, he continued to minister. God helped him to honour his physical body, he learnt to observe his thinking then renew his mind, God provoked him to action and then God moved him back into relationship. Elijah lived on. In fact, what is quite humorous is that Elijah never died, even though he experienced a suicidal episode. How good is that! He went straight up to heaven.

When you feel depressed, it can seem as if you will be stuck in that dark tunnel forever. There are not always quick and easy answers but you are not helpless in the face of depression. There are many steps you can take to help yourself. You can take responsibility for your depression. You can seek to bring it under control and try to control some of the causes. It may take some time to work through your depression but simply acknowledging what you feel and then beginning to take some of the small steps we have shared in this chapter can be very helpful. Freedom is a journey.

One of the most common phrases in the Old Testament is, "It came to pass." The good news about most depression is that it comes to pass. It is not the end. It may be a valley but there is hope. If Elijah was here right now he would probably tell us, "Yeah, I had a really tough time with depression but I found hope and you can too. You can come out of that valley. You can come out of that prison. There is a future for you."

I think that Elijah's story is a terrific example of how we, as church communities, should treat people who are going through a time of depression. God is a phenomenal role model. Did you notice how he treated Elijah? He handled him with care and sensitivity. He gave him encouragement, not just confrontation. Elijah's experience with depression probably took at least a few months of time. This did not all happen in one day. God was very patient in helping Elijah work through and come out of this valley.

I pray that churches will become safer places, so that when people are struggling with depression, followers of Christ will be there to support and help them. I pray that we will be patient with people as they work through what is going on in their life. That is what God desires his community to be.

PRAYER

Depression robs us of our joy, saps us of our energy and hinders us from fulfilling our purpose in life. With God's help, we can be free from depression. Start taking some steps toward your freedom today.

Are you battling with depression right now? Maybe you have been experiencing some low moods. Maybe you have been fighting depression for the last few weeks, months or maybe even years. I pray that you will find hope. Take a step forward today. I would love to pray for you. Receive from God's Spirit even as you read the words of this prayer.

"Father, you see what is happening in our inner world. You see our low moods and all of our feelings. Sometimes we do not understand what is going on. Depression can be very complex and very confusing. Lord, I pray for your grace to come into my friend's heart right now. We pray that you would dispel the clouds and that they would see the light of the sun again. I pray for peace to come into their heart and mind. Help them to give attention to their soul, to what is happening in their inner world. May this emotion of depression be a part of their journey towards healing. May they know the fullness of your joy once again. Amen."

REFLECTION QUESTIONS

1. Have you ever experienced depression? If so, what were the contributing factors? What did it feel like at the time? How did you deal with it?

2. What could you do to improve your physical health?

3. Can you think of any distorted thinking that may be affecting you right now?

4. What is your purpose in life and how could you pursue it more passionately?

5. What are some ways that churches can be safer places of healing for people experiencing different kinds of depression? Also, what are some unhelpful responses to people experiencing depression that we should avoid?

CHAPTER SIX

FREEDOM FROM REJECTION

All of us have experienced rejection in our life at one time or another. It may have been something very minor or it may be a situation so devastating that it affects our whole life. Here are some common examples: you were not chosen to play on a sports team, you were teased during your school years, you were publicly humiliated or embarrassed, you were not given a job you applied for or you were laid off from your job for no good reason, making you feel redundant.

Maybe you have had an experience where people voted against you. Back in 1993, my dad was the senior minister of Waverley Christian Fellowship, a church in Melbourne, Australia, and he felt it was time to pass the baton of leadership on to someone else. He sensed that God's calling was on my life to be the next leader, not because I was his son, but because he felt that it was God's will for the church. The elders affirmed this unanimously. The church constitution required the members of the church to also vote to confirm the appointment of any new senior minister. There were approximately one hundred members at the time and the vote was ninety-eight for and two against. I remember, over the next few days, how I pretty much ignored the ninety-eight and kept thinking about those two people who did not want me, who did not think I would do a good job. I felt a little rejected. Of course, I now realise that this was probably the best vote I would ever have. In life there are always people who may not agree with you or who may not like you.

There are many other more painful examples of rejection. You might have been an unwanted child. Your parents or parent did not plan on having a child, or another child, and then you came along. You may have had a lot to work through because of that. Perhaps you grew up in a home where you never felt loved or accepted. Unfortunately, a lot of parents give their kids food, education and clothing but they may never give them the very thing that they need the most, which is to be loved and accepted. Maybe you never had a parent tell you that they loved you and that you are special. This usually leads to some feelings of rejection. Possibly you had a brother or sister that was always favoured above you. They were always commended and you always felt like you were in their shadow.

Perhaps you grew up in an environment where there was abuse (verbal, physical or even sexual) and that has caused great damage. Maybe you come from a home where your parents divorced and you are still struggling to come to grips with that. You might even be living with one parent who is still working through their own hurt and pain and may not be giving you the love and acceptance that you need. Perhaps you were married once and you thought it would last forever but for some reason it did not work out. You are now divorced and you feel a sense of betrayal and of broken trust. If you have had any of these or similar experiences you know what it is to feel rejected.

UNDERSTANDING REJECTION

Rejection really hurts. It is like a wound on the inside that dramatically affects us. We may even feel crushed. Rejection is very, very painful.

Rejection can be defined as a sense of feeling unwanted. You desire people to love you, yet you believe that they do not. You want to be part of a group, but you feel excluded. Somehow you are always on the outside looking in.

Rejection is one of the most common sources of a host of other personal problems. Rejection is a root from which much that is harmful can grow. Rejection is not outwardly visible. It is more of a hidden, inner attitude that we carry around. That is why we need to see rejection rooted out of lives so that it does not continue to bear negative fruit (Matthew 3:10).

The primary result of rejection is the inability to receive or communicate love. A person who has never experienced being loved cannot give love. The apostle John said this:

We love because he first loved us (1 John 4:19).

When we have received love, it is quite easy to then give love to other people. However, if we have never received love, if we have been rejected, then we will tend to reject other people. We will find it difficult to accept and love others and to receive their acceptance.

People respond to rejection in different ways. Some people go into a tunnel of self pity, despair, and hopelessness. Some people even commit suicide, which is the ultimate statement of feeling rejected and unwanted. Life is no longer worth living anymore. Other people respond to rejection by putting up walls of defence. It may even be a façade of happiness or confidence on the outside but inside they feel hurt and rejected. They do not want to be rejected again so they are not going to let you in or see what is happening on the inside. Other people respond to rejection by becoming aggressive. They go on the offensive and they become angry and resentful. These types of people tend to hurt others. We all respond differently but the end result of all rejection is that we can end up in a prison that holds us back from the life that God has for us.

MY DAD'S STORY

My dad, Kevin Conner, was born back in the late 1920s to a young woman who wasn't married. She didn't want to be pregnant because she didn't have the ability to look after a child. As a result, my dad was placed into a foster home when he was only three months old. He grew up without a father or a mother. In fact, he never met either of his parents. He humorously says that he feels like he was born in a "Reject Shop."

This rejection caused a lot of depression in my dad's early years. Taken from foster home to foster home, he never knew where he was. This created a lot of uncertainty and instability in him. As a result, he clammed up. Like a tortoise he pulled his head in and simply withdrew in order to try and deal with his rejection. They were tough years for him.

Once when he was staying in a Salvation Army boy's home, there was a visiting day, which happened about once a month. Kids who had parents would have their parents come and give them chocolates or lollies. My dad always wondered where his parents were and why they never showed up.

At the age of fourteen, my dad surrendered his life to Jesus Christ at a Salvation Army meeting. He experienced an overwhelming sense of the peace of God flooding into his heart. He realised for the very first time that God loved him and that God accepted him, even if nobody else had.

However, it still took my dad many years to work through his rejection, even after becoming a Christian. People still teased him about his illegitimate birth. At times, he hated himself and wished he were never born. Many times he had suicidal thoughts where he simply wanted to end it all. It was like a constant torment that was difficult to handle.

Later on my dad married and became a father to my sister and I. He prayed that God would turn the negatives in his life into positives. He asked God to help him to be a good father, like the father that he never had. He chose to give us what he never received – acceptance and love. He also became a spiritual father to many. God helped him to start a new generation of those who love God (Exodus 20:4-6). You can read more about my dad's story in his book *This is My Story* (Melbourne, Australia: KJC Publications, 2007).

My dad's journey to freedom from rejection involved a number of ingredients. It included him accepting the work that Jesus accomplished through his death on the cross. He then came to a place where he received God's acceptance of him. He became part of a loving and accepting church family who provided a healing environment. He came to a place where he accepted himself. Finally, he chose to forgive those who had hurt and rejected him. Let's unpack these principles in more depth.

BELIEVE THAT JESUS TOOK YOUR REJECTION

How do you break free from a prison of rejection? First, believe that Jesus died for your rejection. In Christ, God made one all-inclusive provision for freedom from every prison: the sacrificial death of Jesus on the cross. Jesus took our sin, our pain, our shame and our rejection upon himself.

Jesus was rejected by people. This was prophesied by Isaiah who said that the Messiah would be ". . . despised and rejected" (Isaiah 53:3). Jesus spent three and a half years ministering to people. He loved people. He healed people. He spent hours ministering to their needs and setting them free. He did nothing but good. However, in a moment of crisis, the mobbing crowd chose to set Barabbas, who was a rebel and a criminal, free. To Jesus they declared that they wanted him crucified. He did not just have two people vote against him. Jesus had an entire city say that they wanted him dead, although he had done nothing wrong (Matthew 27:22-26). Jesus experienced rejection at a deep level.

Not only was Jesus rejected by people, he was also rejected by his Father. On the cross he cried out:

My God, my God, why have you forsaken me (Matthew 27:46)?

It is hard to understand this because Jesus and the Father are one, but when Jesus became sin for us, his Father turned away his gaze in that agonising moment.

You and I may have experienced some measure of rejection but not to this degree. Jesus understands and identifies with our rejection. Choose to believe that Jesus took your rejection and your pain upon the cross. He did this so that we could be free.

RECEIVE GOD'S ACCEPTANCE

Next, receive God's acceptance. When Jesus died, something dramatic happened. The curtain of the temple was split from top to bottom (Matthew 27:51). This was a highly symbolic act through which God was saying that access into his presence was now open to all. The barrier between God and humanity was torn down. The way was opened for us to come to God without shame, without guilt and without fear. Jesus took our rejection so that we might experience his acceptance. We can now become children of God (1 John 3:1-3).

Come to Jesus and accept him as your Saviour. Ask him to forgive you for the mistakes you have made and for everything you have done wrong. Then receive the acceptance of Father God. You may have had a great natural father or you may have had a father who was not there for you and who may have even rejected you. Thankfully, you can find acceptance in a heavenly Father who is a perfect father.

If you asked me what I think of our three kids. I would, without hesitation, say that I love them and that I think they are amazing. They are the best kids in the world to me. Yes, they have misbehaved and disappointed me at times, but my love for them is constant because they are my children. If I, as a flawed human father, am like this, how much more does our heavenly Father love and accept us as his children!

God's love for us is not based on our performance but on the fact that we are his children. Don't seek significance through your performance or through the approval of others. God has provided for us a sense of love, acceptance and significance apart from our ability to perform. We have been justified or placed in right standing before God through what Christ has done. Of course, now that we are loved, forgiven and accepted we will want to love and obey God – not in order to be accepted by him but because we already are. Believe that Jesus has taken your rejection and receive his acceptance right now.

ENGAGE WITH YOUR SPIRITUAL FAMILY

Third, engage with a spiritual family. God's love for you is not only to be experienced vertically (between you and Him) but also horizontally (between you and others). God wants each of his children in a spiritual family where they can experience love and acceptance. We are brothers and sisters in Christ. Our journey to freedom from rejection includes finding acceptance in a loving community.

We are only complete in relationship with others. Just like the parts of a human body need each other, you need others and they need you. No one is unnecessary. God's family is to be the best family – a place where we experience God's love for us, our love for him and our love for each other. As we learn to fully receive God's love and acceptance for ourselves, we are then positioned to pass that love and acceptance on to other people. By the Spirit, the Father wants to fill our hearts with his love (Romans 5:5).

The apostle Paul tells us that we should:

Accept one another, just as Christ accepted us (Romans 15:7).

Christ accepted us unconditionally, even before we were acceptable. That is the challenge for church congregations today, to be an environment where people are accepted just as they are. Acceptance is not necessarily giving approval of a person's behaviour. However, it is a choice to place value on them and to see them through Christ's eyes. Every person on planet earth, no matter who they are or what they are like, matters so much to God that he sent his Son to die for them.

Let's become a community that welcomes people as they are and then allows Christ's love to change them over time. Acceptance is very powerful. Notice the complete transformation that took place in Zacchaeus' life in response to the loving acceptance of Jesus, despite his infamous reputation in the local community (Luke 19:1-10).

Let's work together to help avoid church communities becoming dysfunctional, where abuse, fear, intimidation and control rule, causing terrible damage to people's lives. Let's seek to make our churches healthy and safe places for people to be, because of the love and acceptance being offered. It is an essential part of everyone's journey to freedom.

ACCEPT YOURSELF

Because God has fully accepted us, we need to also accept ourselves. We are made in God's image and likeness. We are his children. God does not make junk. We are his "masterpiece" – his work of art (Ephesians 2:8-10). This is sometimes the hardest step of all. Begin seeing yourself as God sees you. Base your view of yourself on what God says about you. Declare who you are in Christ according to God's Word. Try to avoid feelings of inferiority (rejection) and of superiority (pride). Begin overriding the old, negative self-talk and start to accept yourself.

Accepting ourselves can be quite a challenge, especially when we realise that we still have faults and that we are still working through various issues. This is not some kind of pop psychology where we stand in front of a mirror and repeat over and over, "I like myself, I like myself, I like myself!" We are talking about accepting ourselves based on the value that Christ puts on us. We can accept ourselves because Christ accepts us, just as we are. That is quite powerful and it is a totally different matter than trying to artificially prop up a superficial sense of self-esteem.

Jesus tells us that we should love our neighbour as ourselves (Matthew 19:19). Jesus assumes that we love ourselves and that we accept ourselves. We should then treat others in the same way. However, if we do not accept ourselves, we will tend to reject others in the same way that we reject ourselves. We simply pass on the rejection we have received. We need to accept ourselves as imperfect, yet a child of God. Then because we are accepted and loved, we can now begin to love and accept other people.

KEEP A FORGIVING STANCE TOWARD OTHERS

Finally, we need to keep a forgiving stance towards those who have hurt us. In response to those who rejected and crucified him, Jesus prayed:

Father, forgive them, for they do not know what they are doing (Luke 23:34).

What an incredible statement. They did not even apologise yet he chose to forgive them. Of course, they would reap the consequences of their actions and if they never repented they would not be forgiven. However, Jesus still chose to adopt a forgiving stance towards those who hurt him.

The apostle Paul tells us that we should forgive other people in the same way that Christ has forgiven us (Ephesians 4:31-32). This can be very difficult because when we are rejected our natural reaction is to feel animosity, hatred and resentment towards those who have hurt us. However, if we give back to people what they give to us, we keep the negative cycle going. Hurt people tend to hurt people. This cycle of hurt and rejection will continue until someone breaks the cycle.

Forgiving those who hurt us and reject us is not an easy thing to do. In fact, it is virtually impossible without God's help. However, the Holy Spirit will give you supernatural grace to do so, if you ask. Forgiveness is not a feeling; it is a decision.

The most powerful evidence that you have been healed of the wound of rejection is that you can love the person who rejected you. This is the most unnatural thing in the world but it can happen through the supernatural power of God's love. In this way, you become a vessel of God's love to others who may have been wounded just as you were. Use an offence directed towards you as a means of reflecting Christ's love back to them.

Is there someone who has hurt or rejected you that you need to forgive? Maybe there is a letter you need to write. Perhaps the person who hurt you has passed away. I read a story recently about a man who had great hatred towards his father because of rejection. His father had died many years earlier. However, he made a courageous decision and went to the cemetery where his father was buried. No one else was there. For a couple of hours he poured out all of his resentment, all of his hurt and all of the poisonous feelings that he had towards his father. He wept uncontrollably and he came to a place where he was able to forgive his father. He left that cemetery feeling totally free. His father never apologised but he needed to get rid of all of that resentment.

Bitterness affects us more than it affects the people who we are bitter towards. You can go through a bitter experience and not become bitter, if you ask God to help you to forgive. Forgiveness is vital if we are to break out of any prison of rejection and live the full life God intends for us.

PRAYER

Following is a prayer for release from rejection. I believe that words are very powerful. God created the world with the words of his mouth. In a similar way, your words can create death or they can create life (Proverbs 18:21). I encourage you to say this prayer out loud and use the words as an expression of your heart. Believe that, as you pray, God will bring freedom to your life and root out any rejection from your past.

"Thank you, Father, for sending Jesus to die for my sin and my feelings of rejection. I thank you for accepting me just as you accept your Son, Jesus. May your amazing love be the foundation of my life. I choose to accept myself and those around me. I choose to forgive those who have hurt and wounded me. I let go of bitterness, resentment and hatred. Help me to love others just as you love me. Thank you for setting me free from rejection – right now, in Jesus name. Amen."

Now here is my prayer for you:

"Father, you heard those words today. Those words have been spoken and there is power in them. I pray that you will set us free from rejection. May our lives be founded in your immeasurable love so that we may become people who know they are loved and accepted by their heavenly Father. Help us not to spread rejection or resentment or hurt to other people. May we spread the love and the acceptance that you have given to us to other people beginning today.

For those who are like my father and who have experienced rejection in their childhood, I pray that you would help them to start a new generation. May they be part of a generation of people who follow God and who are free from rejection, who pass on the blessing of acceptance not the curse of rejection. Give us a fresh start today, I pray, in Jesus' name, Amen."

REFLECTION QUESTIONS

1. Think about a time when you felt rejected. What happened and how did it affect you?

2. What are some indicators that a person is battling with rejection? In other words, how does rejection affect our lives?

3. Why do we sometimes find it difficult to accept ourselves?

4. God loves and accepts us as his children apart from our performance. However, when we disobey him he is not pleased with us and moves in to appropriately discipline us. How do we balance out this sense of always being loved by God yet also being held accountable for our behaviour?

5. What are some characteristics of a healthy family? What are some characteristics of a dysfunctional family? What are some ways you can ensure that your church family is healthy rather than dysfunctional?

6. Do you have a story of someone that God helped you to forgive? What was the impact on you as well as on the other person?

CHAPTER SEVEN

FREEDOM FROM ADDICTION

↑

Addiction is the condition of being enslaved to a habit or practice to such an extent that stopping it would cause severe trauma. It starts with a person choosing to engage in some activity or take in some substance. Initially there is a buzz, a high, and a thrill, and then eventually it becomes a destructive habit or pattern. Over time, it turns into a compulsion where the person is doing it regularly. They begin to arrange their life around it to the point that it becomes an obsession.

The person then starts to experience abnormally strong cravings for this activity or thing. It starts to controls them and they become dependent on it. They can't live without it. It's starting to do damage in their life and in their relationships, yet they continue to pursue it. They are addicted. This is the most reliable sign of addiction - continued involvement in an addictive activity despite negative, life-damaging consequences.

COMMON ADDICTIONS

There are many kinds of addictions in our world today. We immediately think of drug addiction. There are a lot of illegal drugs available today such as marijuana, heroin, ecstasy and cocaine. An increasing percentage of the population has taken an illegal drug at some time into their life. Although there may be a kind of a high from these kinds of drugs, they can do a lot of damage in people's lives and cause addiction.

Another area of addiction is in the area of tobacco or cigarettes. Cigarettes are the most widely used legal drug. Five million people die every year around the world from smoking related causes. In comparison, one million people die from malaria. Smoking is the biggest legal killer in the world today. Thankfully, the percentage of people who smoke is going down each year. However, because of the addictive power of cigarettes, sometimes it can be quite hard to give up. When I travel I sometimes look in the duty free shops and there is always a cigarette section, usually with a large sign that says, "Smoking Kills!" Despite this, there are always people wandering around there and buying cigarettes, because of the power of addiction. When you continue doing something that will detriment your very life, that's an addiction.

Alcohol can become a very addictive substance and that's why some people choose to totally abstain. That's a wise choice. Other people choose to drink in moderation, which is also an acceptable choice to make. Unfortunately, many people drink in a way that harms their life. Here in Australia, thirty-five percent of people who drink, drink at a high risk level that is doing damage to them and their relationships.

Sadly, thousands of people die every year from alcohol related causes.

Another area of addiction is gambling. Billions of dollars are gambled and lost each year. Gambling can take a hold of a person's life and do great damage to them and their relationships. It often leads to depression or even suicidal tendencies. For your interest, your chance of winning the lottery is one out of seven million. You're more likely to be hit by lightning!

Another area of addiction is in the area of sexuality. There's a huge increase taking place in sexual addictions. One of these is pornography, especially internet pornography. Currently, there are over four million web sites dedicated to pornography. That's twelve percent of all of the existing web sites. In fact, it's estimated that one in four, or twenty-five percent, of search engine attempts are related to pornography. The pornography industry is now one of the biggest in the world. If you added up the income of Apple, Microsoft, Google and eBay, the income from the pornography industry is greater than all of them combined. It's worth almost one hundred billion dollars per year. When people become involved in pornography it can become very addictive in their life.

There are also a lot of other somewhat more respectable addictions such as food addictions. Most people love food. In fact, it's estimated that in the western world one-third of people are overweight. Some people eat for comfort. There is also an increase in eating disorders, such as anorexia and bulimia which do cause a lot of damage in people's lives.

Television can become an addiction. It's estimated that the average person watches one thousand hours of TV a year. If you live until the age of sixty-five years old, that means that you will have been sitting in front of the television for almost ten solid years. That's average. In contrast, if you go to church once a week and you live until the same age, you will have only been in church for four months. Never say that church is too long! Watching television can become an addictive activity.

There is now a new addiction called internet addiction, where people are so addicted to the internet that they end up continually surfing and spending far more hours online than they intended to. They're always checking their email and it becomes an addictive activity for them. Then there's shopping addiction. Some people are compulsive spenders. They're already in debt and their credit cards are maxed but they've got to buy that next thing. There's a buzz, there's a high, there's a fix from purchasing that item, even though they don't need it and they're buying it to impress people they don't even like.

Work addiction is another one. We call it workaholism. Not everyone has this. Some people have work aversion and need to get busy working. Workaholism does not mean that you love your work and you're passionate about it. That's okay. Becoming a workaholic is when you're meeting some need in your life and you're working to the point where you're driven. You can never switch off and your work is beginning to damage your relationships.

Exercise can become an addiction. There are many activities and substances that we can become addicted to. We live in a society where there is an epidemic of addictions taking place. Our world is filled with all sorts of cravings, appetites for mood changers and a quick fix mentality that only feeds the likelihood of addictions.

Every one of us, including myself, is vulnerable to addictions. In fact, the worst thing you could do is to skim through this chapter and think that you don't need this. Open up your heart and realise that every one of us are vulnerable to addictive behaviours and we need to be on guard against them.

THE ADDICTIVE CYCLE

Let's take a moment to think about how the addictive process works. James, the brother of Jesus, wrote a letter to some people living in the first century and he said this:

> God blesses those who patiently endure testing and temptation. Afterward they will receive the crown of life that God has promised to those who love him. And remember, when you are being tempted, do not say, "God is tempting me." God is never tempted to do wrong, and he never tempts anyone else. Temptation comes from our own desires, which entice us and drag us away. These desires give birth to sinful actions. And when sin is allowed to grow, it gives birth to death. So don't be misled, my dear brothers and sisters (James 1:12-17).

James gives us some insight into how the cycle of sin or wrongdoing works in our life. It goes like this. We have desires. Some of them are good, some of them are bad. Our desires lead to actions or behaviours aimed at what we think will fulfil those desires. When we choose a wrong action, initially there may be a bit of a buzz that feels really good. But then there is somewhat of a letdown. The consequences do some damage in our life. However, what happens is that our brain tends to release chemicals that reinforce the positive buzz. As a result, when those desires emerge again we do the same thing. Eventually, it forms a pattern and we become addicted.

The problem with addictions is that they offer short term relief (pleasure) but they also create long term problems (pain). The activity becomes an obsession that takes control of our life. That's not a good thing. We don't want to be mastered or controlled by anything. Listen to what Paul has to say about this:

You say, "I am allowed to do anything"—but not everything is good for you. And even though "I am allowed to do anything," I must not become a slave to anything (1 Corinthians 6:12-13).

Even though some activities may be okay or not bad in and of themselves, don't let them become a prison around your life. Otherwise you will become a slave, an addict to it. Later in the same letter, Paul says something similar:

You say, "I am allowed to do anything"—but not everything is good for you. You say, "I am allowed to do anything"— but not everything is beneficial (1 Corinthians 10:23-24).

Paul says that we should make sure that we don't allow anything in our life to become an addictive habit that controls us. Otherwise we become a slave to it and it begins to do damage in our world. The good news is that it doesn't matter what habit, what addiction we may have, there is freedom with the help of Jesus Christ. There are no hopeless situations. Our habits and addictions are no exception. Listen to what Paul had said earlier in this letter:

Don't you realize that those who do wrong will not inherit the Kingdom of God? Don't fool yourselves. Those who indulge in sexual sin, or who worship idols, or commit adultery, or are male prostitutes, or practice homosexuality, or are thieves, or greedy people, or drunkards, or are abusive, or cheat people—none of these will inherit the Kingdom of God. Some of you were once like that. But you were cleansed; you were made holy; you were made right with God by calling on the name of the Lord Jesus Christ and by the Spirit of our God (1 Corinthians 6:9-11).

In many ways this is a very positive declaration. Many of the people that Paul was writing to were caught up in all sorts of life-controlling addictions but now they had been cleansed, made holy and made right with God. They had been imprisoned by a variety of bondages, lifestyles and addictions but now they had been set free. They had broken the power of addiction in their life. This only took place through the help of Jesus Christ. That's good news!

Addictions and some habits can be so firmly established in our lives that they seem to be insurmountable barriers. Finding freedom from addictions is not easy. However, it can be done. It requires a structured strategy, persistence and God's help.

I want to share five very practical principles for breaking free from any addiction in your life. Think about your life. We're all on a continuum of addiction. You may not be addicted, but you may be heading in that direction. These principles will help you find freedom from anything that's taken control in your life.

BE DETERMINED TO CHANGE

First, you have to be determined to change. Obviously that includes admitting that you have an addiction. That can be a challenge and somewhat humbling. There's often fear, shame and guilt associated with addictions. Be honest with yourself and God. Break out of denial. Recognise that what you're doing is wrong or destructive. Often the people around us recognise the problem before we do. However, we are the ones who have to come to the point where we're determined to make a change ourselves.

What you tolerate, you will never change. If you're tolerating that addiction and you want people to leave you alone, you'll never change. You have to come to a point of desperation where you recognise the damage you are doing in your life and you determine to stop what you are doing. The number one reason why people don't break free from addictions is because they try to do so half-heartedly. If you're not serious, if you're not determined to break the power of that thing or that activity in your life, it will never happen. It starts with making a decision. Be determined to change. Focus on the disadvantages of the habit and the advantages of breaking it.

REFLECT ON WHY YOU DO WHAT YOU DO

Making a decision to change is good but will-power is never enough to break the power of an addiction or a habit in life. Will-power will never get you through. It's a good start, but there has to be more. We need to reflect on why we do what we do. It is so easy to focus on the activity or the thing and miss the root cause. The addiction is the symptom. The issue is not the alcohol, the cigarettes, the television or the pornography. Yes, they have an addictive element to them but the root or the source of all addiction is within you. It's on the inside of us.

Think about why you do what you do. Observe your thinking patterns. Most addictions occur because we're trying to gain some pleasure or some satisfaction to fulfil what is missing in our life or we're trying to avoid or alleviate some kind of pain. If you don't take the time to reflect on the inner part of your world, you'll never break the power of addiction. Reflect on what's happening on the inside. What motivates you to do this? What are you looking for? Why are you attracted to this?

It may be an escape from other problems that need dealing with. Get beyond the symptoms and try to understand the root cause. Ask God to show you what need you are trying to meet or what painful emotion you are trying to cover. The source of addiction lies within us. It is our "dis-ease." It is often unmet emotional, social and spiritual needs that cause negative moods and feelings that make us vulnerable to addiction.

EXPECT GOD TO HELP YOU

As you determine to break the power of addiction in your life, expect God to help you. Sometimes we think that God's only around those who are doing well. The truth is that God is near those who are struggling, those who are hurting and those who are in prison. He's right there opening the door and calling you toward freedom. When you make a decision that you want to be free and when you start reflecting on why you do what you do, expect God to be there to help you. He is a friend to the prisoner. He doesn't want you to stay in that prison of addiction. He's got an incredible future for you. Expect God to begin to show up when you get serious about breaking addiction in your life.

We can come boldly to the throne of grace to ask for help in our time of need (Hebrews 4:16). We can do all things through Christ who strengthens us (Philippians 4:13). The very reason Jesus came was to bring freedom to the prisoners (Luke 4:18). You are not on your own. God is with you and for you. Breaking free by ourselves can be virtually impossible but when God is in your life you have a power available to you well beyond your own resources. Expect God to help you out when you get serious about breaking addiction.

ADOPT A STRATEGY FOR STOPPING

Next, it helps to adopt a strategy for stopping. It's great to
make a decision. It's good to reflect. It's good to ask God
to help. However, we also need to translate our decision
into action. We have to change how we are living our
life. Freedom requires both faith and wisdom. This is the
wisdom part. Here is a strategy for stopping that has five
components that will help you put a plan together for
breaking the power of the addiction.

ABANDON FOOLISH THINKING

First, abandon foolish thinking. When we are addicted, our
thinking becomes twisted. A sort of deception comes over
us. We begin to maximise the pleasure, the payoff we're
getting, and we minimise the consequences. That's absolute
foolishness. We've got to start renewing our mind and
embrace reality thinking. We need to begin looking at the
reality of the consequences of our lifestyle.

If you continually look at pornography, how will that
affect the way you relate to people? How will it influence
your relationships? What kind of a person will you become
as a result? If you keep watching TV hour after hour, what
is your life going to show when it's all over and done? If you
keep gambling your money away, what's going to happen?

Start by beginning to change your thinking. The apostle
Paul tells us that we are transformed by the renewing of
our mind (Romans 12:1-2). We need to abandon foolish
thinking. We've got to look beyond the baits. All sin, all
addiction, has a pleasure element but the pleasure only lasts

for a season. We've got to look to the consequences. We've got to look at the end result.

Think past the high to what you'll get afterward if you give in. Focus on a negative memory or ugly reminder of your addiction, rather than dwelling on pleasant memories. Reject the lie and believe the truth. Meditate on God's Word in order to cleanse your ways and purify your habits. Remind yourself of the gains you are moving toward by breaking free from your addiction.

Recovery is about finding more real gratification and pleasure in life, not less. However, this is not found in people, possessions or circumstances outside of ourselves but through a relationship with God who longs to live inside of us. What is the source of your happiness? Who do you trust for real life? Find inner contentment in Christ (Colossians 2:9-10).

DISTANCE YOURSELF FROM THE ADDICTIVE ACTIVITY

Second, distance yourself from the addictive activity. Decide to make a complete break and get out of the addictive loop. Don't keep flirting with an activity. It only keeps the cravings alive and makes relapse inevitable. Like an allergy, you need to avoid the irritant.

The more distance you can put between you and your drug the more likely you will abstain. Don't be strong, be smart. Run from temptation, don't have a discussion with it (1 Corinthians 6:18, 2 Timothy 2:22). No temptation comes our way that we can't conquer and from which God promises to give us a way of escape (1 Corinthians 10:13). If you want to quit smoking, get rid of all your cigarettes and the ashtray.

If you want to break an alcohol addiction, get rid of all the alcohol.

Most addictions are broken through total abstinence. Don't try to wean yourself off pornography. Make a complete break from it. Obviously, with some addictions total abstinence may not be appropriate. If you've got a food addiction, you can't stop eating. However, you can stop overeating. If you've got a workaholic tendency, don't stop working. However, you can begin to adjust the amount of time you're giving to work.

OPEN UP TO HELPFUL PEOPLE

Thirdly, open up to other people who can be of help to you, including your family and friends. It's very hard to break an addiction on your own. When you're on your own, you're isolated, you're lonely, and you tend to sink into a mire of self pity. That's why we need community. That's why we need friends.

Most people benefit greatly from a strong healthy support network to help them break the power of addiction in their life. Don't try to go it alone (James 5:16). Helpful people include mature Christian friends, prayer partners and a qualified counsellor. Form healthy relationships and make yourself accountable. Open yourself up and move from isolation to community.

PROTECT YOURSELF FROM POSSIBLE TRIGGERS

Fourth, protect yourself from possible triggers. Avoid high risk situations. Catch the addictive activity before it starts and be on guard for the times and situations when you are most likely to carry it out. There may be places that you need to avoid. If you are struggling with alcohol, going down to the pub is probably not the best idea. The very smell of the place would be a trigger to your addiction.

There may be some people that are triggers. I was talking to a woman recently from our local community. She has struggled with addictions for many years but through the help of our church's counselling ministry, she has found freedom in her life. One of the things she had to do in her journey to freedom was to pretty much cut off all of the relationships in her life down to only two people. That was really hard but it was essential as so many of her friends at that time were only encouraging her to continue in her addictive lifestyle. If she hadn't done that she would have never broken free.

Sometimes we have to make some tough choices. Perhaps it is moving house or changing a phone number. We have to protect ourselves from any place or person that is going to trigger and draw us back into the lifestyle we're trying to get out of.

It may be a mood. Certain moods make us vulnerable to our addiction. It may be feeling down or feeling tired or feeling a little depressed or a little anxious. It could be a mood that draws us back in. We need to recognise this and run from temptation in order to protect ourselves from those various triggers. Be alert to the promptings of the Holy Spirit and obey them.

TURN YOUR FOCUS TO ALTERNATE POSITIVE THINGS

Fifth, turn your focus to alternate, positive things. Replace the addiction with alternative behaviour. Find something else to do instead. Develop good habits of behaviour to replace the old patterns. Put on a new way of living to replace what you want to put off (Ephesians 4:22-32, Colossians 3:8-10). This is so very important. Breaking free from addiction is not just about getting rid of the negative. It's about putting the positive into our life.

If you've been lying, then stop lying and start speaking the truth in your conversation. If you've been stealing, stop stealing and start working so you have some money to give away. If you've been speaking a lot of negative words, gossip and tearing people down, then stop that and start speaking words that build people up. The way you break the negative is not to yell at the darkness but to turn the light on.

Structure your time, especially your free time. Get involved living your life for others. When you genuinely get involved in assisting others in any way, it helps you to not be obsessed with your own issues. Resurrect your dreams! Start making some long-range plans. Establish some clear direction and goals for your life.

Many people stay in their prison of addiction because they've got no dreams, they've got no goals and they've got no future. The truth is that God has a future for every one of us. He has plans for us and they are to give us a future and a hope (Jeremiah 29:11). The goal of your life is not freedom. Freedom is simply the foundation from which to live a life of purpose. Your purpose in life is not getting out of prison. Prison is the place that the enemy's been trying to get you into in order to kill your purpose (John 10:10). One of the keys in breaking addiction is to lay hold of something better to live your life for.

Wendell Smith, one of my youth pastors when I was in high school, used to say the greatest deterrents to sin is not rules but vision. If you start to find a vision for your life, you'll start realising that certain things are not going to help you get there. In fact, they will ruin your potential. So you start to get rid of them because you're going somewhere with your life.

If you're struggling with addiction, it's time to begin to resurrect your dreams. God's got a future and a hope for you. It's not just about freeing you from the addiction. It's not just getting you out of the prison. It's about getting you back on track with God's purpose for your life.

KEEP BELIEVING FOR COMPLETE VICTORY

The final step in breaking free from addiction is to keep believing for complete victory. This is so vital. Never give up! Trying hard for one week will not bring about long-lasting change. It is not easy and at times you will feel discouraged and want to give up. You may get tired of trying to break free.

Any time a person starts to break an addiction, they need to expect some withdrawal symptoms. When a person has been addicted to an activity or substance that's had an effect on them physically and psychologically, this is inevitable. If you are a coffee drinker, have you ever tried to have a complete break from coffee? Any time you change a process or a way of living, there's always some withdrawal symptoms. It may be headaches or sleeplessness or a loss of energy. We need to understand that these withdrawal symptoms are temporary. They're not permanent. Realise that they are going to happen and push through them into the new life God that has for you.

Not only will there be withdrawal symptoms, there will be cravings. You can stop the activity or habit but those cravings will emerge. Again, they are only temporary but if you don't push these cravings away in the first couple of weeks of breaking free, you'll fall back into the addiction again.

Push through the withdrawal symptoms and the cravings. Otherwise you'll end up relapsing. Many people who try to break addictions do well for a while and then they fall back into the previous behaviour. You might have heard the funny quote by Mark Twain who said, "Quitting smoking is easy. I've done it hundreds of times."

Stopping an addiction is one thing, staying free from an addiction is a totally different matter. If we don't realise that we've got to push through some of this rough water, then we set ourselves up for disappointment. A lapse is a dangerous thing, because we engage in the activity again which suddenly reinforces all the old patterns and cycles. However, a relapse does not mean that it's over. The writer of the book of Proverbs tells us that even a righteous person may stumble seven times but they get up again (Proverbs 24:16).

Determine to rise up and continue to press on. Keep believing for complete victory. Never give up. You may stumble. Learn from it. Ask yourself why it happened. What was taking place? Go through the process. Continue to believe for complete victory. Don't allow failures to discourage, frustrate or disillusion you. Learn from them and move on.

When you are addicted it's like walking down an escalator that's going down. The escalator is moving downward and you're walking down with it. It's almost pulling you down. If you want to break the addiction, you can't just stop. If you just stop, you'll still go down because the pull is there. You have to turn around and begin walking upwards and while you're walking upwards, the pull, the escalator, is still going the other way.

When you are breaking an addiction, you may have stopped but realise that the pull is still there. You have to keep walking against it in the new opposite direction. Over time, that pull will gradually diminish and eventually it can go away and you're into complete freedom. However, if you don't walk through that transitory season, you're going to be pulled back down and you'll be trapped by the addiction once again.

FREEDOM FOR THE PRISONERS

The good news is that Jesus came to bring freedom for the prisoner. I believe that he can help us to break free from any addiction in our life. That's his purpose for us.

One final thought related to addictions. One day God was talking to Jeremiah, a prophet who really felt God's heart. He told Jeremiah:

My people have done two evil things: They have abandoned me—the fountain of living water. And they have dug for themselves cracked cisterns that can hold no water at all (Jeremiah 2:13)!

God declares himself as the source of living water that alone will satisfy humanity's deepest need but they've forsaken him. In replacement, they've created some other containers that really don't hold life-giving water. In fact, they run empty and they never satisfy.

Ultimately, every addiction is an idol in our lives. There is a need in our life or a pain in our heart and we are looking to that thing to fill the void, quench the pain, or meet the need. We're looking to something other than God. That's what grieved the heart of God in Jeremiah's time. They forsook him and became involved in all sorts of other things that never really satisfied.

Addiction never delivers what it promises. That's the story of the human race. In the beginning we have a perfect world. Adam and Eve are in harmony with God and they're satisfied. However, the enemy begins to capitalise on their cravings and offers them something other than a relationship with God. It was a fruit tree and they went for it, thinking that it would satisfy. Did it? The rest is history. What a mess it's been since then.

Fast forward a couple of thousand years. Jesus, the son of God, has been fasting for forty days. He's hungry. He's got some cravings. Once again the enemy comes in to capitalise on his cravings and to tempt him to fulfil them in a way that was not legitimate. Jesus, unlike the first Adam, didn't give in. He overcame the temptation of the enemy. The great news for us is that Jesus Christ, if you're a believer, now lives inside of you and he can help you to overcome temptation too.

Addiction always involves a lie. It offers us a way to meet a need that only God himself can meet or heal a pain that only God can heal.

Paul tells us that we are complete or whole in Christ (Colossians 2:10). We live in a world that tries to make us think that we're not adequate, that we need to buy that, we need to do this, or we need to look like this. It's trying to feed our addictive tendencies. The truth is that in Christ, we are complete. We have the source of living water. Jesus is the source of true living water. When we are full of his life, we enjoy life but our source is in him.

PRAYER

Is there an activity or a substance that is starting to take control of your life? I pray that some of these principles will be able to help you to find freedom. Have the courage to deal with your issues. Don't ignore them thinking they'll go away. More often than not, they only get worse. If you are doing well, I encourage you to be on guard. We are all vulnerable and we should be aware that we have a spiritual enemy who tries to offer us a lie. Continue to draw on the life that is in Jesus Christ.

Here is my prayer for you:

"Father, I pray for each person reading this book. Thank you for their humility and their honesty to admit that something in their life may be starting to take control.

May they be determined to make a change. Help them to reflect on why they do what they do. Show them if there is an inner need or a pain that they're trying to avoid. Show them what's happening in their inner world. Come alongside them and give them power to do what they cannot do in their own willpower alone. Father, give them a strategy. Help them to keep believing for complete victory, to push through the withdrawals and the cravings and maybe even a lapse. May they stand up once again. Break the power of addiction in their life by your Spirit, in Jesus' wonderful name. Amen."

REFLECTION QUESTIONS

1. Have you ever experienced freedom from any sort of addiction in your life? What happened and what were some of the keys to finding freedom?

2. Read James 1:13-15. What are some ways that we can learn from our mistakes so we don't keep repeating them (Proverbs 26:11)?

3. How can we be a support to those struggling with addictions of any kind?

4. Read Colossians 2:9-10. How can we find greater fullness in our relationship with Christ so that the allure of other things becomes less attractive to us?

5. Pray for strength to conquer any destructive habits or addictions in your life.

CHAPTER EIGHT

FREEDOM FROM SPIRITUAL BONDAGES

↑

If you've ever read through one or more of the Gospels, you'll have discovered that in addition to teaching, making disciples and healing people, Jesus spent considerable time freeing people from the influence of demons or evil spirits (Luke 4:31-37, 41). Jesus came to invade the kingdom of Satan and free those held captive. This often led to a dramatic spiritual confrontation between the powers of darkness and light.

As you move into the book of Acts, you'll notice again that in addition to teaching, making disciples and healing people, the apostles and early church leaders also spent time helping those influenced by evil spirits to find freedom (Acts 5:12-16).

We should do the same – go about doing good, teaching, healing, and helping people find freedom from the work of the enemy. In fact, at the end of his gospel record, Mark quotes a teaching of Jesus that seems to make this a normal part of every Christian's life:

Then (Jesus) told them, "Go into all the world and preach the Good News to everyone. Anyone who believes and is baptized will be saved. But anyone who refuses to believe will be condemned. These miraculous signs will accompany those who believe: They will cast out demons in my name, and they will speak in new languages. They will be able to handle snakes with safety, and if they drink anything poisonous, it won't hurt them. They will be able to place their hands on the sick, and they will be healed (Mark 16:15-18)."

Even though this statement is not included in some of the earliest manuscripts of the Gospel of Mark, it does reflect both the ministry and teaching of Jesus and the practice of the disciples as recorded in the Book of Acts in the New Testament. Jesus' desired that people be set free from demonic oppression and added to the kingdom of God.

When you read a story of demonic deliverance in the Bible it raises a lot of questions such as: How did this person become possessed? When did it happen and how long had it been? Where did this demon go? What are demons anyway? Are they real? Are demons still around? Can demons influence Christians? How would we know if one was around anyway? What would we do if we became aware of one?

A THEOLOGY PRIMER:
SATAN AND DEMONOLOGY

Let's put those questions aside for a moment and do a quick overview of what we do know or assume about Satan and demons from the Bible.

In addition to the creation of myriads of angels, God also created archangels. We have the names of three of them in the Bible – Michael, Gabriel and Lucifer. Michael appears in the books of Daniel, Jude and Revelation and he seems to be over the armies of heaven. Gabriel appears to Daniel, Zacharias and Mary and seems to be God's messenger especially about the Messiah. Lucifer is referred to in Isaiah 14 (though the NIV translates his name "morning star") and Ezekiel 28. These passages were addressed originally to the kings of Babylon and Tyre. However, in their long-range implications, many scholars believe, they refer to Satan himself.

Lucifer may have been in charge of the worship in heaven. Yet something rose up inside of him that wanted to be worshipped, just like God. In his pride, he lifted himself up against God and led a revolt in heaven. As a result, he and one third of the angels were cast out of heaven. This beautiful archangel, who was created by God, became the Devil. Many believe that these fallen angels became demonic spirits.

The Devil is also referred to as Satan, in addition to accuser, deceiver, tempter, ruler of this world, god of this age and prince of the power of the air. The first place we see him on earth is in the Garden of Eden (Genesis 3:1-

15). He comes in the form of a snake, a symbol of cunning and deception. He tempts Eve and both Adam and Eve end up mistrusting and then disobeying God, bringing a curse on themselves and the entire planet.

One of the curses was that there would be continual enmity or warfare between Satan's offspring and the seed of the woman (Genesis 3:15). The seed of the woman would one day crush Satan's head but he would bruise his heel. In the Old Testament we see Satan appearing a number of other times, including in the book of Job and references to evil or lying spirits influencing and using people for his purposes.

Jesus' ministry began with forty days in the wilderness where he was tempted and tested by the devil, who desired worship. Satan left him for a while but then came at other times to try to trick him off course, even placing thoughts in Peter's mind aimed at trapping Jesus (Matthew 16:21-23). Much of Jesus' ministry involves freeing people from the influence and control of demons who have been sent by Satan to do his bidding.

When Jesus taught his disciples about prayer he included this aspect in his teaching:

Don't let us yield to temptation but rescue us from the evil one (Matthew 6:13).

Satan tried to trip up Peter, but Jesus prayed that his faith would not fail (Luke 22:31). Satan entered inside of Judas and influenced him to betray Jesus then take his own life (John 13:27). On the cross, Jesus defeated Satan and completed the work of redemption.

The apostle Paul tells us that we are in a spiritual battle between the kingdom of light and the kingdom of darkness (Ephesians 6:10-18). We live in a parallel universe and there is interaction between the natural and the spiritual worlds. We are not to be unaware of Satan and his schemes (2 Corinthians 2:11). Satan can even appear as an angel of light (2 Corinthians 11:14). In fact, his main power over us is deception. Paul himself had received a "thorn" in the flesh, which was a messenger of Satan to attack him but God had given him grace to overcome (2 Corinthians 12:7). Paul says that God will crush Satan under our feet shortly (Romans 16:20).

James says to submit to God, to resist the devil and he will flee from us (James 4:7). Peter tells us that Satan is like a roaring lion seeking who he may devour (1 Peter 5:8-9). We need to resist him.

Satan is an undercover agent. You probably won't see him but behind every temptation is the tempter, behind every lie is the father of lies. For example, he tempted Ananias to lie to the apostle Peter about the profits of a property he and his wife had sold (Acts 5:3). Behind every seduction is the seducer.

In the Book of Revelation, we see Satan and his angels at war with Michael and his angels in a great cosmic battle. Michael wins and Satan is bound in a deep pit for one thousand years. He is then loosed and cast with all his demons into a lake of fire, where he will be punished forever and ever. Amen. So the good news is that in the end we win. That's if you're on God's side, of course!

AVOIDING EXTREMES

So how do we respond to all of this? I believe that there are two extremes we need to avoid. First, we should avoid a preoccupation with Satan and the demonic world. Some people know and talk more about the devil, demons and spiritual warfare than they do about God and the gospel.

People who go to this extreme see a black cat and think the devil must be on the prowl today. There is an overcast day and they think there is an oppressive spirit over the city. Someone coughs and they quickly say, "Come out!" They have a tough week and they tell you that the devil has been chasing them. They make a mistake and they say that the devil made them do it. They meet a woman with a strong personality and they declare that she has a Jezebel spirit. They're feeling down so they pray against a spirit of depression. Someone acts cool to them and they think that they better watch their back. You get the picture. We could call this person Demonic Dave.

Second, we should avoid being ignorant of or full of unbelief in relation to Satan and the demonic world. Some people, including Christians, live like the devil doesn't even exist. Back in the 1970s, Christian artist Keith Green sang a song from the devil's perspective called *No One Believes in Me Anymore* which emphasised how easy it is for the devil today to work his tricks because so few people believe in him.

People who go to this extreme think that everything can be understood through reason and science. They believe that God is real but they are not sure about the devil and demons. They think the demonic realm is a lot of hocus pocus. When bad things happen, they see the cause as bad luck, change, or coincidence. To them everything has a logical explanation. We could call this person Sceptical Susan.

Where would you be on this spectrum? Are you more like Demonic Dave or more like Sceptical Susan (with apologies to all the Dave's and Susan's reading this book)? Which way do you need to move?

I don't believe that followers of Christ can be demon possessed, as God owns us. However, demons can influence Christians both externally in the form of various attacks (oppression, affliction, torment) and internally if we give them a foothold through various access points. How do I know this? Read what the apostle Paul had to say to the church at Ephesus:

> So stop telling lies. Let us tell our neighbors the truth, for we are all parts of the same body. And don't sin by letting anger control you. Don't let the sun go down while you are still angry, for anger gives a foothold to the devil (Ephesians 4:25-27).

The word "foothold" refers to a place, an opportunity, or adequate room to move. It's like a door or an opening that gives access to demonic influence. We can think of a computer that needs virus protection or a house that is only safe if its doors and windows are locked.

Paul tells us not to give place to the devil, which means it's obviously possible. If we give ground to the devil, we can give demons the right to occupy parts of our lives, like illegal squatters. At times people have to be loosed or set free from demonic involvement.

What are some possible access points for the enemy to work in our lives? I'm sure there are many and it's worth giving this some serious consideration. Let's look at four possible access points for demonic influence from my observation, experience and study.

INVOLVEMENT IN THE OCCULT

Involvement in activities such as the occult and false religions is not only offensive to God, they can open us up to the influence of the evil one and therefore need to be renounced (Deuteronomy 18:9-14). This includes a whole range of activities from extremes such as Satan worship, witchcraft and séances through to involvement in magic, fortune-telling, palm reading, tarot cards and astrology. Involvement in various cults or secret societies also needs to be renounced.

Here is an account of what happened at the church in Ephesus back in the first century:

God gave Paul the power to perform unusual miracles. When handkerchiefs or aprons that had merely touched his skin were placed on sick people, they were healed of their diseases, and evil spirits were expelled.

A group of Jews was traveling from town to town casting out evil spirits. They tried to use the name of the Lord Jesus in their incantation, saying, "I command you in the name of Jesus, whom Paul preaches, to come out!" Seven sons of Sceva, a leading priest, were doing this. But one time when they tried it, the evil spirit replied, "I know Jesus, and I know Paul, but who are you?" Then the man with the evil spirit leaped on them, overpowered them, and attacked them with such violence that they fled from the house, naked and battered.

The story of what happened spread quickly all through Ephesus, to Jews and Greeks alike. A solemn fear descended on the city and the name of the Lord Jesus was greatly honored. Many who became believers confessed their sinful practices. A number of them who had been practicing sorcery brought their incantation books and burned them at a public bonfire. The value of the books was several million dollars. So the message about the Lord spread widely and had a powerful effect (Acts 19:11-20).

When we become Christians, through the cross there is provision for complete wholeness and freedom. It is similar to every chain being unlocked and every prison being opened. However, we need to apply the power of the cross in our life and go free from things that have held us captive.

A good example of this process is the resurrection of Lazarus. Jesus raised him from the dead by the power of his word. However, his friends and family had to untie the grave clothes from him once he came out of the tomb. In some ways this is a picture of our freedom. We receive new life through Christ but we often need untying from various things that have had a stranglehold on our lives.

These believers in Ephesus confessed their sin. They then removed everything related to their former way of living from their life. I believe we should do the same – renounce and remove.

NEGATIVE GENERATIONAL INFLUENCES

The affect of sins from previous generations can also influence us if they are not renounced (Exodus 20:5-6, Nehemiah 1:6, John 9:2, 2 Corinthians 5:17). This does not take away personal responsibility and we can begin a new godly generation through appropriating the work of Jesus on the cross.

As part of the giving of the Ten Commandments, Moses told Israel that sins and their affect could be passed on the succeeding generations (Exodus 20:4-5). This does not mean that we are doomed to repeat the mistakes of our ancestors nor does it mean that we don't have the power and responsibility to make right choices today. However, there is no doubt that behaviour tendencies can be passed on from generation to generation, for good or bad, and the enemy likes to take advantage of this.

The Old Testament story of Achan demonstrates how one person's sin can affect not only themselves but also their family and many others (Joshua 7:1-26). Another example of this belief was seen when the disciples assumed that a man born blind may have experienced this as a punishment for his parent's sin (John 9:1-2). They understood generational sin, although in this case Jesus made it clear that this was not the cause and that his sickness would be used to bring glory to God (John 9:3).

Around the beginning of the twentieth century, a Mr. E.E. Winship published two studies of two well-known American families of the nineteenth century. His findings have been published in many publications since that date and are well worth considering.

Max Jukes was an atheist who married a godless woman. Some 560 descendants were traced. Of these: 310 died as paupers, 150 became criminals, 7 of them murderers, 100 were known to be drunkards, and more than half the women were prostitutes. In all, the descendants cost the U.S. government one and a quarter million nineteenth century dollars.

Here we clearly see the possible roots of destructive behaviours in families. A strong negative influence can pass through the bloodline of those who hate God. The good news is that the blessings of God are also passed on from parents to the next generation. What a wonderful heritage and inheritance children can receive from godly parents.

Jonathan Edwards was a contemporary of Max Jukes. He was a committed Christian and married a godly young lady. Some 1394 descendants were traced. Of these: 295 graduated from college, from whom 13 became college presidents and 65 became professors; 3 were elected as U.S. senators, 3 as State Governors and others sent as ministers to foreign countries; 30 were judges; 100 were lawyers, one the dean of an outstanding law school; 56 practised as physicians, one was the dean of a medical school; 75 became officers in the army and navy; 100 were well-known missionaries, preachers and prominent authors; another 80 held some form of public office - 3 were mayors of large cities; one was the comptroller of the U.S. treasury and another became a vice-president of the United States. Not one of the descendants of the Edwards family was a liability to the government.

Although the historical accuracy of some of the statistics in this study has been called into question in recent times, it nonetheless highlights how real and powerful generational influences can be - for good or for evil. However, they can be broken. Through Jesus Christ we can begin a new godly generation no matter what our family tree is like (2 Corinthians 5:17). We can set up the next generation for success in God, though we cannot make their choices for them nor be responsible for those choices.

PERSONAL SIN

Sin, which is disobedience to God's instructions, can also become an access point to the enemy. When we repeat sin it can easily become a habit or a pattern in our life. These habits then become ingrained and become weaknesses or areas of vulnerability. Satan knows how to take advantage of these and he often uses them as access points. Sometimes this leads to addictions or compulsive behaviour where we feel like we can't even stop ourselves.

An example of this is Judas whose uncontrolled greed and love for money caused him to be vulnerable to the entrance of Satan into his heart. This led to his betrayal of Jesus for thirty pieces of silver he never lived to spend (Luke 22:3). In a similar way, the apostle Peter discerned that Ananias' subtle lie was a result of Satan filling his deceptive heart (Acts 5:1-6).

Another illustration is in the area of our sexuality. Sexual attraction is normal but not every attraction is appropriate. We need to control inappropriate sexual attractions, whether we are single or married. When we don't, we give in to lust.

Lust can become a habit, if we are not careful and can even turn into an addiction which can potentially open a person up to a spirit of lust. At this stage the lust turns into an obsession where there is almost a complete loss of control and an inability to stop. It is the same with anger which, at its extreme, can give way to a murderous spirit. In saying all of this, let's not become a Demonic Dave. We need to keep a balanced view on the demonic but we must not underestimate the destructive power of sin in our lives, especially when it is not repented of and allowed to become a recurring pattern.

Confessing and forsaking our sin is vital (1 John 1:9-10). Sin is living life contrary to the way God designed us to live. It offends God, it causes damage to us and other people, and it gives the enemy an opportunity to take advantage of us. No wonder the writer of the book of Proverbs says:

> People who conceal their sins will not prosper, but if they confess and turn from them, they will receive mercy (Proverbs 28:13).

PERSONAL HURTS

Personal hurts are unhealed wounds from the past that may come from things such as abuse, rejection and unresolved conflicts. Our natural response is anger, hatred and bitterness. However, these things tie us up on the inside, sapping the life out of us and giving potential access to the enemy. That's why Jesus tells us very clearly to forgive those who have hurt us, lest we open ourselves up to spiritual torment (Matthew 18:34-35).

As we have already seen, unresolved anger can give the devil a foothold in our lives (Ephesians 4:27). However, with God's help we can forgive those who have offended us, releasing them to God who is just, ensuring we keep ourselves free from spiritual bondage.

HOW TO EXPERIENCE SPIRITUAL FREEDOM

Please notice that these are possible access points. Just having one or more of these conditions in your life does not automatically mean that you are being influenced by demonic spirits any more than leaving your door unlocked in your home means you've been robbed. However, we need to be on guard.

What do we do if some of these access points are relevant to our lives? Do we need deliverance ministry? Sometimes that can be necessary but more often than not we can find freedom in Christ through some simple steps. We start by doing what is necessary to close these access points up.

Demonic spirits can be likened to flies or rats, in that they're attracted to wounds and garbage (rotting things). Instead of swatting at the flies or yelling at the rats (the symptoms) and causing quite a commotion, it is wiser to seek to bring healing to the wound and to remove any garbage that may be attracting them (root causes). If you do this effectively, you'll find that the flies and the rats will disappear without much of a fuss. I believe that this is a much more balanced approach to this important area of ministry.

Freedom from spiritual bondages sometimes occurs instantly through the power of the Holy Spirit. At other times it takes a process of time, which may include renewing our mind, finding healing for our emotions and strengthening our will. Our goal should be to ensure that there is nothing whatsoever in our lives that has the potential of becoming ground on which the enemy can occupy and do his destructive work.

My desire for you is not to create fear in your heart but rather to create awareness so we can know the full freedom that Christ desires for each one of us. Like Jesus, may we be able to say:

The chief of this godless world is about to attack. But don't worry — he has nothing on me, no claim on me (John 14:30. The Message Bible).

PRAYERS OF FREEDOM

Our words are very powerful. God created the world with his words. Although we are not God, we are made in his image and our words have great power – to either cause death or life (Proverbs 18:21). I am going to encourage you to say some freedom prayers about each of the areas we have shared about in this chapter. I believe that if you will say this from your heart and with conviction you can know a greater degree of spiritual freedom beginning today.

Let's make some declarations and draw a line in the sand. We are fully aware of the devil and his devices. We want to let him know that in Christ we will defeat him and we will experience full freedom in our lives. I believe that by doing this a spiritual transaction can take place. Then from this moment on we need to maintain our freedom. This may require some specific actions on our part.

Following is a prayer of surrender to God followed by prayers of freedom for each of the four possible demonic access points discussed in this chapter. Make them a faith declaration and believe for God's Spirit to move in your life and bring you into freedom in whatever area you may be bound.

Surrender: "Heavenly Father, I come to you in Jesus name. I confess that I have sinned against you. Jesus, I thank you for dying on the cross for me and I accept you as my Saviour. I invite you now to be the Lord of every area of my life – Lord of my mind and all my thoughts, Lord of my emotions and all my feelings and reactions, Lord of my will and all my decisions, Lord of my body and all my behaviour, Lord of my spirit and my relationship with you, Lord of my time, my work, my home, my family, my possessions and all my relationships. Thank you that your blood was shed that I might be set free. Amen."

Involvement in the Occult: "Heavenly Father, I renounce all involvement in the occult, in various cults or in false religion. I renounce any group, practice or belief that does not glorify Jesus. I confess Jesus Christ as my Lord and Saviour. I will serve Him only. I now declare that Satan has no legal right to have any foothold in my life. I claim the release and freedom promised by Jesus Christ. The past is dealt with. My future is assured. Today, I will enjoy the abundant life that is available to me in Christ. Thank you for your righteousness, your peace and your joy. Amen."

Negative Generational Influences: "Heavenly Father, I confess and renounce every sin that my parents or my ancestors may have committed which has brought bondage or domination to my life, and I ask for forgiveness and cleansing. In the name of Jesus I break every curse or sinful tendency that may have been passed on to me from my family or previous generations. I am now in Christ and I have begun a new godly generation. I thank you that Jesus took every curse for me on the cross of Calvary. He died and then rose again so that I might be completely set free. Amen."

Personal Sin: "Heavenly Father, I repent of every sin, wrong action or attitude. I ask you to forgive me. Cleanse me and wash me completely. Thank you that you have now forgiven and forgotten my sins. They are dealt with and covered by the blood of Jesus. Thank you for your mercy. I now choose to forgive myself for the things that I know you have already forgiven me for. I now turn from my sin. Give me discernment to recognise temptation when it comes and the strength to resist it. Amen."

Personal Hurts: "Father, I confess that, as a result of being hurt, I have allowed myself to hold anger, resentment and bitterness in my heart. I acknowledge this as sin and I now repent and turn from this behaviour. Thank you Jesus for dying that I might be forgiven. By an act of my will I now choose to forgive those who have hurt or offended me. I release each and every one of these people into the freedom of forgiveness and I refuse to hold on to any bitterness or resentment. Amen."

REFLECTION QUESTIONS

1. Do you think there is too little or too much emphasis on the devil and the demonic today?

2. Do you know of anyone that has been influenced by demons?

3. Paul warns us not to give the devil a foothold (Ephesians 4:27). What do you think about the four possible access points presented in this chapter? Can you think of any others?

4. In this chapter, demons were likened to flies in that they're attracted to wounds and garbage. Instead of swatting at the flies and causing a big commotion, it is wiser and more effective to help bring healing to the wound and to remove any garbage that may be attracting them. Dealing with symptoms without getting to the root cause is not helpful. What do you think of this word picture?

CHAPTER NINE

WHEN FREEDOM ELUDES US

↑

The message of this entire book is good news. We can be set free from every prison that surrounds us, whether it is a prison of worry, anger, fear, depression, rejection, addiction or spiritual bondage. Jesus came to set the prisoners free. He came to break every chain. He came to release every captive into the full life that he desires for us. We can experience a prison break. Yes, we can be free.

Is this really true? Can this really happen – in every person's life and in every situation? Is this too ideal? Can these promises become a reality? If so, why aren't more people walking in freedom? Is it their fault? What about the contradictions of life? What about when things don't work out the way we want them to? What about when life doesn't give us the happy ending we were hoping and praying for? These are all good questions and we need to pause and reflect on them.

SUFFERING

One area of life that often affects our ability to find freedom is that of suffering. We live in a fallen world. As a result, we all experience difficulties and even times of contradiction when life doesn't make sense. Suffering touches every one of us.

Consider the story of Job. He was a good man who lived a life of obedience to God yet he experienced intense suffering. He went through incredible grief and deep depression. At times he wished that he had never been born and wanted his life to end. His friends started out well by offering sympathy to Job for his many calamities but then they started accusing Job, assuming that because bad things were happening in his life, he must have done something wrong. If he was truly righteous before God, he would be blessed.

After a long period of time, God vindicated Job's innocence. He delivered him from his suffering and restored him to a life of blessing. However, let's not forget the long valley of darkness that Job went through. His faith was tested to the very core because the circumstances in his life didn't make sense. Even after the difficulties ended, he still had to work through the grief of losing his loved ones.

David was a man after God's own heart yet he struggled with the contradictions of life. At times the wicked were prospering and the righteous were doing it tough (Psalm 73:1-20). Was it really worth serving God? Shouldn't life be easier? He battled with all sorts of negative emotions, including fear, worry, grief and anger.

The three Hebrew children faced potential death in a fiery furnace because they would not bow down to a foreign god. Would God deliver them? Would he protect them? Their faith was strong enough to handle any result. Here is what they said to the king:

> If we are thrown into the blazing furnace, the God whom we serve is able to save us. He will rescue us from your power, your Majesty. But even if he doesn't, we want to make it clear to you, your Majesty, that we will never serve your gods or worship the gold statue you have set up (Daniel 3:17-18).

They believed that God was able and that God was willing to save them but even if not, they would still serve the God they worshipped. What great faith. We also need an "if not" in our faith so that we can handle times of difficulty and hardship.

Many of the heroes of faith listed in Hebrews 11 had incredible answers to prayer and deliverance from painful situations. However, there were "others" who for some reason didn't see their prayers answered in this life. Yet they were still honoured as men and women of faith who loved and served God even through the contradictions of their lives.

> How much more do I need to say? It would take too long to recount the stories of the faith of Gideon, Barak, Samson, Jephthah, David, Samuel, and all the prophets. By faith these people overthrew kingdoms, ruled with justice, and received what God had promised them. They shut the mouths of lions, quenched the flames of fire, and escaped death by the edge of the sword. Their

weakness was turned to strength. They became strong in battle and put whole armies to flight. Women received their loved ones back again from death.

But others were tortured, refusing to turn from God in order to be set free. They placed their hope in a better life after the resurrection. Some were jeered at, and their backs were cut open with whips. Others were chained in prisons. Some died by stoning, some were sawed in half, and others were killed with the sword. Some went about wearing skins of sheep and goats, destitute and oppressed and mistreated. They were too good for this world, wandering over deserts and mountains, hiding in caves and holes in the ground.

All these people earned a good reputation because of their faith, yet none of them received all that God had promised. For God had something better in mind for us, so that they would not reach perfection without us (Hebrews 11:32-40).

Jesus in the Garden of Gethsemane cried out for his Father to take away the cup that he was about to drink (Matthew 26:39). If there was another easier road to take, he was keen to take that. He knew that his Father cared for him. He knew he was able to remove this cup of suffering but in this case he didn't take it away. Humanly speaking it looked like God was not being fair. However, God's higher purpose was the redemption of us all and we're glad that he had his Son drink that cup and go to that agonising death on the cross. Jesus submitted himself to the will of his Father, even though that required him to experience suffering and pain.

When we experience suffering in our lives it can seem like a prison. We feel confined and restricted. Suffering can also affect us emotionally and we become more prone to negative emotions such as worry, fear, anger, and depression. However, it is possible through God's grace to avoid allowing these to take hold of our lives. Even in the midst of difficulty and contradiction, it is possible to experience joy in God, knowing that he is in full control and will work all things out for our ultimate benefit (Habakkuk 3:17-19. Romans 8:28. Philippians 4:4)

THE NOW AND NOT YET

On the cross Jesus conquered Satan, sin, sickness and death. He said, "It is finished", and it was (John 19:30). However, we live in the time of the end, which involves a tension between what theologians call the "now and the not yet."

"Already" Satan has been conquered. He is a defeated foe but "not yet" has his final judgement taken place. In between, he continues to try to deceive the nations and we have to resist him.

"Already" sin has been atoned for. Forgiveness is freely available but "not yet" do we see sin totally eradicated. Sin has to be fought like a deadly virus and repentance is the vaccine that releases forgiveness and freedom.

"Already" sickness has been defeated. However, "not yet" do we see sickness and disease totally removed from the earth. Also, any healing is not permanent. As far as we know, all people who Jesus healed eventually died. Sometimes God heals and sometimes he does not. Jesus did not heal everybody. No one can give any fixed answers as to why. Only God knows. Our responsibility is to pray and ask God to heal and help us (James 5:13-16), then to trust God with the outcome. Our attitude is not one of fatalism but one of faith.

"Already" death is defeated but "not yet" do we see death destroyed. Our bodies are all ageing and unless Jesus returns beforehand, we will all die. We are all getting older each day. All of us will die of something, until Christ's return for that generation who escapes death (1 Thessalonians 4:15-18). Death is the last enemy to be destroyed (1 Corinthians 15:21-28).

The contract has been signed and paid in full but we are living in this in-between time before what has been legally accomplished on the cross becomes a complete reality. There will come a day when Satan and his hoards of demons will be judged and cast into a lake of fire for eternity. Even now, his time is short. There will come a day when sin will be cleansed from the earth and from our lives. There will come a day where sickness and pain will be no more, where suffering ceases. There will come a day when death, our last enemy, will finally be destroyed. That day is the second coming of Jesus Christ.

So the kingdom of God is both present ("already") and future ("not yet"). Until then, we stand firm and we fight against all that the devil seeks to bring against us. That's why we continue to pray, "Your kingdom come. Your will be done (Matthew 6:9-15)." This prayer is a request for God to reign and to manifest his sovereign power by putting to flight every enemy of righteousness. Understanding the reality of the "now and the not yet" is important in our fight for personal freedom.

THE GOD OF THROUGH

It would be great if God would deliver us from every difficult situation immediately. None of us like to have to go through times of challenge and pressure. It's not pleasant and it's not easy. However, we need to understand that God is a God of "through". Listen to what the prophet Isaiah had to say about this:

> But now, O Jacob, listen to the Lord who created you. O Israel, the one who formed you says, "Do not be afraid, for I have ransomed you. I have called you by name; you are mine. When you go through deep waters, I will be with you. When you go through rivers of difficulty, you will not drown. When you walk through the fire of oppression, you will not be burned up; the flames will not consume you. For I am the Lord, your God, the Holy One of Israel, your Savior (Isaiah 43:1-3).

I wish it said that God always delivers us "from" the fire and from the deep waters. At least it could say that God takes us "around" these situations , or "over" these things or "under" these difficult times. No, it says God at times takes us "through" fires of oppression and rivers of difficulty. That is a wonderful promise but it is also a good reality check that helps us adjust our expectations about what life will be like here on this earth. Part of our prison break may involve walking through that prison for a while until we get out the other side.

SUFFICIENT GRACE

The apostle Paul had what he described as a "thorn in the flesh (2 Corinthians 12:7)." Scholars have debated for centuries as to what this "thorn" was. Some believe it was a sickness, possibly an eye condition (Galatians 6:11). Others think it was a particular person or group of people, such as the Judaisers, who were giving Paul much difficulty and opposition (Galatians 6:12-13). The fact is that we don't know what it was but we do know that it was painful and irritating to Paul. It tormented him.

Three times Paul prayed fervently, begging the Lord to take it away. In each case, God answered him and said:

My grace is all you need. My power works best in weakness (2 Corinthians 12:9).

Here is a situation where Paul did not receive the answer to his prayer that he desired. He was not freed from this thorn. However, God did provide more than enough grace for him to endure its pain and continue to be effective in life and ministry.

Sometimes life is like that. We'd like to be totally free of everything that seeks to hinder or limit us but sometimes we have to live as "wounded healers", a phrase from Henri Nouwen. We are weak yet through Christ we can be strong. We are wounded yet God's healing can still flow through us to others. That is the paradox of the Christian faith. We have a great treasure on the inside of us but we are fragile clay vessels (2 Corinthians 4:7). The power is from God, not ourselves.

This should not discourage or overwhelm us. If anything, it should lead us to a greater dependence on God. Without him we can do nothing (John 15:5). It is only as we are daily connected to Christ that his life can flow through us helping us to live fruitful lives (John 15:1-5). Even while still in the process of breaking out of whatever prison we may be in, God's grace is available to us.

ARE THEY STILL THERE?

John Forbes Nash was born in 1928. Before long, his parents realised that they had a child prodigy in their hands, a maths prodigy. He had a brilliant mind but was inept socially. He was a bit of an odd ball.

Later in life, he married and then went through a very painful battle with schizophrenia. Towards the end of his life, through treatment and through recognition of his condition, he was able to work through his challenges. In 1994, he earned a Nobel Prize for economics. He was a unique man.

Hollywood made a film of his life called *A Beautiful Mind*, starring Russell Crowe. Towards the end of the film there is a brilliant scene, Nash has come to grips with his schizophrenia and how it affects him. He and his friends are walking along and they're talking about his condition and how he has overcome it. At one stage you will see him

PRISON BREAK
↑

glancing to the side and you will see three figures, a little girl, a man in a black hat and a blonde man. These people are not real. They are figures of his imagination that have haunted him for so long.

Here is the dialogue:

John Nash: "I was thinking that I might teach."
Martin: "A classroom with fifty students can be daunting for anyone, John. Besides, you're a terrible teacher."
John Nash: "I'm an acquired taste, Martin. I was hoping there still might be something I could contribute."
Martin: "What about the – well you know? Are they gone?"
John Nash: "No. They're not gone. Maybe they never will be. But I've gotten used to ignoring them and I think, as a result, they've kind of given up on me. I think that's what it's like with all our dreams and our nightmares, Martin. We've got to keep feeding them for them to stay alive."
Martin: "John, they haunt you though."
John Nash: "Well, they're my past, Martin. Everybody's haunted by their past. Well, goodbye."
Martin: "John, I'll talk to the department."

Isn't that just like our life at times? Worry, anger, fear, depression and even addictions try to torment us. We have a choice each day as to whether to feed them or not. I wish that all of these enemies would totally disappear but in certain situations, their shadows remain. We decide whether we are going to move towards them and let them influence us or whether we are going to believe the word of God that we can be free from their power.

My prayer for you is that you will find freedom in every area of your life. In the journey towards that goal there may be times of contradiction, difficulty and even suffering. However, I truly believe that God's grace is more than enough to bring us through. We can know his love, his peace, and his joy even in the midst of a prison or in the process of us breaking out to freedom. Together, through the power of Jesus Christ, let's continue to make a prison break in every area of life and endeavour to help other people do the same.

FOR FURTHER READING

Adrenaline and Stress by Dr. Archibald Hart (Nashville, TN: Thomas Nelson, 1995)

A Woman's Guide to Overcoming Depression by Dr. Archibald Hart and Catherine Hart Webber (Grand Rapids, MI: Revell Publishing, 2007)

Healing for Damaged Emotions by David Seamands (Colorado, CO: David C. Cook, 1991)

Learned Optimism by Martin E. P. Seligman (New York, NY: Pocket Books, 1990)

Love is a Decision by Gary Smalley and John Trent (Nashville, TN: Thomas Nelson, 2001)

Managing Your Mind by Gillian Butler and Tony Hope (New York, NY: Oxford University Press, 2007)

The Anxiety Cure by Dr. Archibald Hart (Nashville, TN: Thomas Nelson, 2001)

The Search for Significance by Robert S. McGhee (Nashville, TN: Thomas Nelson, 2003)

Unmasking Male Depression by Dr. Archibald Hart (Nashville, TN: Thomas Nelson, 2001)

Willpower's Not Enough: Recovering from Addictions of Every Kind by Arnold M. Washton (New York, NY: Harper Books, 1990)

ABOUT THE AUTHOR

Mark Conner has been involved in church leadership for over three decades. He is a gifted leader, author and speaker who brings a wealth of wisdom and life experience to whatever he engages in.

In early 2017, Mark transitioned out of the senior minister role of *CityLife Church*, a large multi-site church in Melbourne, Australia. He is now giving himself to training, writing and coaching others toward greater fruitfulness.

Mark has a genuine love for people and a passion to help them grow and change. He has a Masters of Arts degree in Theology from Ridley College in Melbourne, Australia and a Doctor of Ministry degree from Fuller Theological Seminary. Mark is married to Nicole and they have three adult children.

Made in the USA
San Bernardino, CA
25 March 2018